Tracking Pioneers

By

Solveig McCormick

A Family Saga

## Author's Note

This Book has been based on people who have made up several generations of a family, gathered from different parts of the world, that met and married, had children who went off and met and married, and so on through the years. The original focus was on Ivor McCormick and his twin Graham (alias Bob) McCormick and how they fared during World War Two; one in North Africa, RAF and one in Burma, KAR.

Genealogical searches cannot provide more detail than births deaths and marriages. Only one journal covering three years was found, that of Ivor. A news cutting about, and a single letter written by Graham, hiding among possessions, were found after Ivor passed on. These together with remembered conversations that were communicated, based on somewhat hazy memories of details; are not the stuff of fully correct representations of the lives we are recording here.

After much consideration I have generated fictional sub-stories based on ideas of what may have happened, to flesh out the characters, and their histories in an empathetic manner, commemorating all in a loving way. Ever conscious that living family members may not agree with what has been written, I apologise in advance for perceived errors and fabrications of events recorded; largely in the absence of correct information. All errors are of my making, in spite of efforts via research; to create an interesting biography of a fascinating family.

This Book: "Tracking Pioneers"; is dedicated to my children, Patricia and Sean, and their father Alan who has been a great support throughout.

This first edition was written and completed between March 2022 and February 2023.

ISBN: '978-0-6397-6611-9

Copyright ©Solveig McCormick 2023

Solveig McCormick claims the right to be identified as the author of this work in accordance with the Copyright and Patents act of South Africa

Grateful thanks to

Melissa Webster
who started me on this journey through her AWA course.

http://www.storiesandvoices.org

## TRACKING PIONEERS – A PROLOGUE

In the wilds, herbivores migrate over large distances seasonally in search of food and water. Herds move in great numbers and as they travel, they leave behind them temporary wastelands. Different animals feed on varieties of natural vegetation. As the land is denuded, they leave behind them myriads of tracks that would be visible from the air. As they defaecate, they enrich the earth. Nature is a healer generally, and seasonal weather repairs the temporary desertification, allowing the herds to trek back to where they were the year before. The self-preservation instinct is the impetus of migration, in any species.

In farming practice, a man with herd animals will create a rotational grazing system which gives paddocks a chance to recover, so that there is always sufficient food available. Where there is a nature reserve, the game keepers will also intentionally practice nature preservation techniques.

Birds annually migrate vast intercontinental distances, defying human capacity to absorb the possibility. Various human tribes are nomadic due to the seasonal climatic conditions, and the sensitive nature of their environment. Some humans carelessly destroy their surroundings in seeming ignorance. Others have learned that the earth needs to be cared for and nurtured, not raped and plundered. Life is a process of moving on, and learning continues as we progress.

From time immemorial human cultures have travelled for exploration, out of curiosity or for trade, or to seek a better land that offers a richer survival prospect. Then there are the conquests where one nation plunders another for gain or domination. This is the stuff of history.

This story about to be told is of the gathering of individuals from one part of the world to another for various reasons, and how people met and married and nationalities and histories intermingled as men and women married and then, for one reason or another, moved on seeking a better life for their children.

They left behind their mementoes of themselves, as they travelled forwards developing new lives, and further enriching generational history. No matter who we are, or what we do, we leave something of ourselves behind as we move on, captured in the memories of people that we have loved or who have loved us. Sometimes we are not even aware of the impact we have had on our immediate society. We leave tracks behind us as we continue pioneering into new lives.

## Chapter One
## About Alan - The Year 1975

*"O fear not in a world like this,
And, thou shalt know erelong
Know, how sublime a thing it is, to suffer and be strong"*

*Longfellow – The Light of Stars*


In Durban, on the East Coast of South Africa, where the deep, dark blue Indian Ocean breakers roll against the white shores, two young people happened to cross paths many times, without noticing one another or meeting by introduction. He was Alan McCormick a part-time University student, also working with Howard Slater's Quantity Surveying offices. On the opposite corner, from Slater's office, Solveig Jacobs was a cashier in a Building Society. They discovered that they had regularly passed one another in the busy city street, and thought it was ordained therefore that they should meet. They had been hitherto merely nameless faces, often seen but not observed.
In the evenings she took a bus to her family residence, disembarked at the top of the hill and walked the short distance home. Almost daily a motorbike flew past, the wind whipping against her, the bike rider's hair, a generous thatch, flying out behind him from under his helmet, literally sweeping her blonde hair awry, exhaust fumes

blowing warm against the stockings on her legs. The risk he took skimming past her this way, rattled her somewhat. Perhaps he was looking for a reaction by regularly doing this but she was not quick on the uptake and only skipped to the side of the road for safety. Should she have yelled and waved? Was that what he wanted? Fifty-odd years later, this has only recently occurred to her. There are times in our lives when we are quite dense.

Time passed and she moved to the city and shared a flat with a friend on the beachfront. This enabled her to spend evenings after work swimming at the Olympic size, saltwater Municipal pool. Daily she worked at increasing the number of lengths swum, until she managed to complete one hundred laps regularly without resting, at each session. She loved walking and swimming and enjoyed the increasing strength of her body.

Her parents were regular attendees at a church so it was a good place to meet them weekly for a "catch-up". One Sunday evening at the Frere Road church, her father called her over and introduced her to a long-haired young man dressed alarmingly in a floral frilled shirt, and purple bell-bottomed trousers. Raised in a convent and by a very strait-laced mother, this apparition was too much for her. His name was Alan. She greeted him politely and excused herself, wandering off vaguely, muttering about needing to get the bus home.

A couple of evenings later she met him again. In the intervening days, he had had a haircut and was dressed for work in what was known in those days, as a safari suit. She was impressed. This most particularly, when due to heavy rain outside, he was encouraged to hang his damp shirt on a chair for a while to dry. After a shaky shy start, a few evenings were spent together in the company of friends. On these occasions, they went out in his rather large and battered gold-painted car, which he called the "old tank". Therefore, she did not make the connection between him and the crazy biker.

She visited the house he was sharing with his friends near where she had been living with her parents, and suddenly; the puzzle pieces came together. It was he who had swept past on the motorbike in the afternoons! They had been close neighbours for a while! He shared what they called a "mess" with a group of several young men, and the house had a swimming pool. So, she went there for a few afternoon or evening swims. Even after all these years, she remembers one of the young men holding a fluffy white cat aloft over the water; and being amazed that the cat was undeterred by this.

Deductions also show that at some point he had met her father, possibly on the road they both travelled and had visited their family home and fallen in love with the beautiful birds in her father's aviary. "Pop" had some wonderful East Asian, unique pheasants, with splendid showy crests and magnificent tails. While she admired them, there was something in her that was repelled by these glorious birds being caged. She had once observed the two of them out there, enjoying the birds, without paying any attention, while she was busy in the kitchen preparing a tea tray to share with her mother. Both of them had left the house at different times in opposite directions, she to meet her bus, and him to join his friends at the commune alias "mess". She wonders lately if her father had taken a shine to Alan and was plotting a touch of matchmaking.

At times while relaxing together, Alan dazzled her with stories of life in Rhodesia. Alan spoke of the wild country and his observations of animals. He loved the cheeky vervet monkeys, the stately Kudu and the graceful Waterbuck with the circle on their rear ends. He talked of close encounters with Elephants, Buffalo, Lions and Leopards. He described the dozy Rhino lumbering along with poor eyesight, which occasionally charged at something or someone having been startled by a sudden movement that caught the eye. It was surprising how these heavy prehistoric beasts with short stubby legs, could gather up a lumbering yet silent-footed run, at an alarming speed when this happened. Despite herself, she dreamed of experiencing these things.

She eagerly anticipated weekends, hoping to "be taken on a date" only to discover that he had gone biking "up the coast" to St Lucia to be in the wild. Or off to the Drakensberg mountains on hikes. This irked. She wished he would invite her along although now all these years later, she understands the impracticality of it. In any case, he talked often about another lady he was seeing. She should have "heard the warning bells" but has sadly been hearing impaired (and somewhat inattentive) for most of her life.

In childhood, her parents had from time to time trundled off, with her sitting in the back of the old Volkswagen "Beetle", up to the Natal Lion Park. Here, almost tame hand-fed lions lay in the sun and gazed in boredom at passing vehicles. Occasionally a Kudu was sighted. Once a young one approached the car and when her father offered a treat of sorts, (which was not allowed) the Kudu nibbled on it, then startled, accidentally catching a horn inside the car. There were a few tense moments, while her father gently helped the Kudu to free himself, before he galloped away. These few events in her life couldn't possibly compare with Alan's exciting animal and bushveld stories.

Then Alan moved to a decrepit old house in the semi-industrial section of the city near the railroads approaching the Station. He and his friends were seriously cutting costs. Her flat share on the beachfront ended, and she moved to a studio apartment on the Southeastern, opposite end of town, almost at the edge of a beautiful, lush green city park, and near the yacht club. Conveniently, it was within walking distance of her workplace in one direction and in the opposite direction, towards where Alan was then living. So, after periods of not seeing him by invitation, she would walk over unannounced to his "digs". The poor fellow was probably feeling hounded.

## Chapter Two

## Solveig's Solidarity

*"The star of the unconquered will, He rises in my breast, Serene and resolute, and still, And calm, and self-possessed."*

*Longfellow – The Light of Stars*

Now all of her teen years, as a result of reading books her mother had collected, she learned of the relatively recent history of the Jews and their survival of life in the ghettos enduring pogroms before, during and after the Second World War. There were stories describing the horrors endured by people in concentration camps, and the escape of many women and children who walked over the Alps through Switzerland and then down the length of Italy, to ultimately board an old cargo skiff. This vessel chugged across the Mediterranean Sea her decks laden with human freight. It was prevented from docking in Israel by the British colonists for many weeks, and at one point was sent back to Italy where the would-be immigrants were temporarily detained in holding camps similar to those they had been fleeing. After a time, they were allowed to attempt immigration again. Yet the British colonists, afraid of Arab reprisals afterwards, held them off the coast for a time, refusing them access to Haifa Harbour for many days. Finally, the seriously weakened, dehydrated people were allowed to dock. But from there, the occupants were kept in a "temporary holding camp" similar to those in Europe from which they had been escaping, situated in the coastal town of Netanya, just south of Haifa. It was the ultimate horror that modern-day Sabras are still upset about. Solveig was taken to see the place and has never forgotten her shock. While living in Israel, she met some of those survivors of the Exodus. The heroism and determination she learned of through her reading, and the viewing of an emotive film called Exodus, whose theme song she trilled endlessly all through her youth, enthralled her with the ideals of Socialist Zionism and the rebirth of the Holy Land. Naturally, actually meeting survivors bearing tattoos on their arms lent emotive value and veracity to what she had read.

She read of the Russian emigrants that arrived in twos and threes, having escaped the cruel pogroms, having travelled overland with basic implements, and started digging desert soil and planting trees at the turn of the twentieth century. From the Jordan River, they dug channels to water their projects. She was increasingly beguiled by the heroism of the beleaguered ghetto dwellers from Russia and Poland. The collective farm was a system they had been accustomed to in the countries they had escaped from. And they recreated it in their new land.

She dreamed of the Zionist movement and of working on a Kibbutz, as well as doing some touring in Europe while in the Northern Hemisphere. These stories still thrill her to this current time.

Previously she had toured for a few months with her sister Ingrid, with a low-cost camping company. They had had so much fun, but her experience of all the history and art, architecture and culture, had only whetted her appetite for more. And of course, part of the tour included trips to see concentration camps and gas chambers. To this day she is appalled by these horrors. She was earnestly saving up as much as possible monthly, towards her personal Israeli adventure.

Meanwhile, her feelings for Alan were deepening and she began to hope for a marriage proposal. She knew that he planned to return to Rhodesia and when it became evident that the proposal was not imminent, she booked her flights, steeling herself to be brave and simply carry on. The planned trip to Israel was her emotional escape plan. As a young child, she had learned that the only way forward in life was to grin and bear the situation.

Now Alan was keen on motorbike off-roading, and motor car racing and had acquired a box of bits of an Austin Healey Sprite, the one with the frog eye lightbulbs. So, he spent every available spare moment on building the car. His friends often wondered if he would graduate given how little time he spent at lectures, or seemingly never having taken notes during lectures that were attended. What we now know is that he is a man of superior intellect and had already acquired adequate knowledge in practical application.

In hindsight, perhaps she was too much of an irritating hanger-on, a distraction; since her admiring presence, loitering and chatting in the workshop, seldom elicited a response. He was not in any way ready for a serious relationship. She was unaware of the bush war to which he would be returning. He had major commitments to his country and the Government Department where he was employed. He was expected to work out the time during which his Ministry had sponsored his studies. Oh, the narrow, near-sightedness of immature female youth!

All too soon he packed up his little vintage sports car, attached a trailer behind it, loaded his motorbike and set off on the epic road trip back to Salisbury.

With mixed feelings of excitement for her adventure to Israel, and disappointment realising that she would never see Alan again, Solveig resolutely boarded her ELAL flight and went to the Holy Land.

## Chapter Three
## Glaswegians

*"Not enjoyment and not sorrow is our destined end or way;*
*But to act that each tomorrow,*
*Find us further than today."*

*Longfellow – A Psalm of Life*

In the closing few years of the 19$^{th}$ century, young Andrew and his twin sister Lillian McCormick, born in September of 1878, sailed from Glasgow to Liverpool, and onwards towards America with their parents, Alexander McCormick and Mary McCormick neé McNiven. It happened thus: Pappa Alexander McCormick farmed generational family land bordering the overcrowded, industrially burgeoning, and rambling town of Glasgow. Having worked with his father in his youth and after marriage, the farm had become his upon his father's death. Recent successive years of heavy rain and excessive cold had blighted his potatoes and rye crops. His cattle had suffered related hoof diseases, and life had become a struggle.

Regular farm assistants had left agricultural work in favour of the many city-related, industrial opportunities that were opening. These were replaced by unreliable day workers who often arrived late in the morning, heavily overhung tending to belligerency, and recalcitrant. Generally, the life of a farmer had become untenable. Pervading pollution filling the air around Glasgow, and general poverty-related, spreading diseases, meant that his young children were always poorly with stomach ailments and persistent coughs.

Too often Alexander arrived home in the evening wet through and laden with stinking mud on his boots in the evening, to find mayhem in the home. His sweet, pretty wife Mary, would be shuddering and dissolved in tears, hair bedraggled, face blotchy, dinner still in preparation while she struggled with children that were yet again feverish and mewling, refusing to eat the semolina pudding she had made for them. The kitchen range would be almost invisible behind lines of damp washing hanging to dry in the steamy kitchen. She could never complete her chores in the house. The weather was terrible and the pretty, "once upon a time" green and pleasant farm, had become a quagmire. The fowl yard near the kitchen was putrid. Leafy vegetables in the kitchen garden developed mould and Mary could not believe the way her sweet, rosy dreams of marriage had turned into such a sour reality. Her life was increasingly out of control and depressing. Had she really fallen in love with this damp and muddy man, with rough hands and a shaggy mess of red curly hair?

Alexander looked sadly at his lovely wife. She had changed from the beautiful fresh-faced girl he had wooed and won.

He remembered walks with her on the moors and clifftops in the springtime. Her blue eyes danced and her lovely smile showed the whitest of even teeth. Her light chestnut hair was always escaping the confines of the chignon she rolled its thick masses into. Her fair skin was rosy-cheeked and silky, like rich cream on the top of the milk. For him, she was a lovely subject, looking for a famous artist to depict in gloriously created and mixed pigments. He wondered if little Lilian would have the same magical aura. Where had all the sweetness and romance gone? How did this grumpy, exhausted young woman, resemble the sweet maiden he had fallen in love with?

Life had become untenable and Alexander began to consider a change, to search for a better life in the New World. At the local, on the rare occasions that he had met other farmers to talk "shop" or rather land management and animal diseases over some Guinness, there had been discussions of opportunities in the Americas where cities were developing on the foundations of industry and further afield, the countryside was experiencing vast agrarian development. He began to dream. He was not sure if he was attracted to big city development. As a farmer with generations of land work and animal husbandry in his history, Alexander was yearning for vast open spaces and sunshine, ripening acres of corn and wheat, with fat dairy cattle grazing contentedly on green meadows. He was not sure that he could tackle road building and bricklaying and quarrying and shipbuilding, or whatever other hard labour was involved in the development of industries in a rapidly growing city. He had seen enough of that here at home in Glasgow. He was a man of the land, bred, born and raised! He just needed to escape this perpetual winter weather that had locked in on Northern Europe for several years unremittingly.

The city of Glasgow was the teeming centre of the industrial revolution. Textile weaving became mechanized which put many women out of work. Great mechanized looms were in manufacture and use. The process of mechanized yarn spinning on a large scale, changed the face of production, and people began to expect to be able to own the newly affordable, refined linen fabrics of higher quality; rather than the unique home-spun and woven wool and heavily textured linens of yore. The port of Glasgow received bulk cotton and dry tea leaves from the East and blending houses sprung up. Bulk wheat was shipped in from Canada and America, and the new industrial flour mills produced large quantities of sifted white flour for the fine pastries, loaves of bread and cakes, that the wealthy enjoyed.

Metalworks raised a generation of mechanics and engineers for the building of railway locomotives, steamships and sturdy metal farm implements. Early developed motor vehicles and trams vied with horses, carts and carriages. The combined stench of horse manure in the street, with various pollutants related to the industries, as well as the "horseless carriage" exhaust fumes, were overpowering. The city grew apace as it drew people searching for work. The air was foul with pollution. Sickness afflicted her inhabitants regardless of income purely because of overcrowding and lack of fresh air. Impoverished children suffered stunted growth in workhouses and long hours of brutal labour; which shortened the life spans of young and old alike. The proliferation of whisky distilleries also contributed to the roughening of society with easier access to the national favourite tipple.

Simply living in this environment had become damaging to the general population's health. The 19th century witnessed major Typhus and Cholera outbreaks in Glasgow as elsewhere, affecting rich and poor alike. These were the result of foul midden ditches behind the rows of houses. Air quality was bad due to industrial pollution and coal fires, which is why the middle classes migrated up-wind to poorer living conditions. Even in the 1890s, one in seven babies died in Glasgow, mainly from the common diseases of childhood such as measles and smallpox. Most families, be they rich or poor, experienced tragedy and grief arising from the death of children or the loss of a parent; while children were still young. In an age that recognised death through elaborate funerals and complex mourning rituals, the death of a loved one could impose a major financial burden on a family and the shame of a pauper burial was keenly felt.

A national survey of 1902 revealed that Glasgow was the most overcrowded city in Britain and the situation became worse in the first decade of the new century as slum clearance was not matched with new home development. Inevitably, therefore, domestic and family life was a constant struggle to keep tidy and well-organised, when there was no space for clothing or possessions and when furniture used for seating during the day had to be converted into sleeping accommodations at night. Housewives were constantly "picking up" and "putting away" simply to keep themselves and their families functioning in the limited space they had available.

Maintaining basic cleanliness was an endless struggle when homes were overcrowded and plumbing was primitive. The pressure on working-class mothers was considerable and it is not surprising that men found the pub a welcome refuge from the daily chaos of domestic life. The middle-class woman found life much easier but even in this privileged group, ideals of domesticity were not always possible in tenement dwellings where privacy was extremely limited.

## Chapter Four

## New Beginnings

*"Let us then be up and doing, With a heart for any fate. Still achieving, still pursuing, learn to labour and to wait."*

*Longfellow – A Psalm of Life*

Oft of an evening, as Alexander cuddled his twins, telling them stories based on traditional legends, and sang to them in his rich baritone the songs his mother had sung to him and his siblings, he started dreaming of a way to make the move to the great open spaces and new opportunities in the Americas. He ardently longed to see his children healthier and his lovely, overburdened wife happier. They talked about it often at night in their bed when the children were asleep. The dream began to fill their thoughts and slowly plans were formed.

Alexander offered the farm to his younger brother Jeremiah who until then had always grumbled about not having inherited land from their father. But by then Jeremiah was involved in mechanical works at the harbour, earning a solid and regular wage, with a promise of pension at the end of his service, and demurred. Neither did his sister and her husband, now living in Edinburgh where he was a banker, and she a teacher of music. Struggling on the land was considered beneath them.

Alexander talked of his dreams to go to the "New World" one evening at the local where he was relaxing with his Guinness. He mentioned his concerns regarding the cost and how the whole transaction could be organised. A couple of days later a smartly dressed man with a briefcase arrived at the farm, in a dray drawn by magnificent matched Clydesdales. He lifted his bowler to Alexander and asked if they could speak. Hesitantly Alexander who had just completed milking and turned the cattle out into the fields took him to the house, busy wiping his hands. They went into the parlour where there was, fortunately, a laid fire that needed only to be lit. Mary brought through a tea tray and then took the children out to feed the chickens and collect eggs.

Hugh McCulloch was a man from the City Offices. He had heard that the McCormicks could be planning to sell their land and he was prospecting for land for a suburban residential extension. The city needed to spread to accommodate its rapidly growing population attracted by all the commercial development. Would Mr McCormick be willing to sell his farmland to the city? Mr McCormick thought that indeed he might if the price were right. He excused himself and called Mary to the kitchen door to ask whether she would like to have a changed life. Yes, she would!

The business was soon settled and berths were found on a ship sailing to New York City. Her name was Great Western and she was a metal double-hulled, single-enginned and smoke-stacked steamship, boosted with masts and sails. The journey was expected to take about sixteen to twenty days weather permitting. Being of a very economical mindset, they paid for a single cabin below decks. This was only for sleeping they reasoned, and in daylight, they could walk about on the deck to take the air. They bought two sea trunks and packed their best clothes and linen, abandoning anything that had only a limited lifespan left. Nestled in the one trunk amidst other treasures, was the inherited family Bible. Excitement mounted as the departure date approached.

Finally, the big day arrived and they embarked. Alexander and Mary hugged one another as they each held a twin and stood on the deck watching all the loading activity from the wharf into the ship's hold. They could not remember when last it was that they had felt so positive and hopeful of the future. How could they know that life is seldom plain sailing? God above tests us to strengthen us.

Finally, the ship's horn blasted her departure warning, and people who had been on the dock delaying final separation parted from their friends and families and the "late arrivals" dashed on board. The gates closed and the ship, tooting her horn slowly moved away from the quayside. There was a good deal of weeping and handkerchief and hat waving as the people on land grew smaller and smaller with increasing distance. Finally, the cold wind drove them below deck laughing uproariously as they struggled to find their sea legs. They stopped in at Liverpool to take on cargo and coal and another family bound for an adventure in America.

There was much seasickness. The sea was rough and the ship ploughed through high waves, climbing up and crashing down again into troughs, with water splashing onto the deck and running off again as the ship rolled from side to side between the waves. This was no modern-day cabin cruiser for the rich. Sea sickness and unsuspected communicable diseases on board the ship, below the decks, meant that some did not arrive alive, failing as a result of extreme dehydration and related debilitation. Thus a few people were buried at sea after an outbreak of fever spread among the passengers, and delirium brought on fits where the seizures resulted in death by suffocation. Nobody traced which passenger had boarded with the fever, ultimately infecting several.

Alexander and Mary, with the twins, went into self-imposed quarantine and kept as much to themselves as possible; only going above deck in the early morning and around sunset, where they would not be crowded, and hoped to avoid infection. Passengers using "below decks" accommodation, were travelling second class, and as such enjoyed different meal times with simpler meals. This meant that they did not suffer excessive seasickness due to eating rich foods and drinking wine. However fresh fruits and vegetables were rare. Inadequate ice crates meant that food spoiled and resulted in upset stomachs. But they received ale rations for good health.

In the final days of the journey, Mary who had thought she might be pregnant and was secretly delighted with the idea of another baby to be born in the new world was however suffering a heavy load of morning sickness. The rolling sea and stale air below decks, where they were, however sheltered, from the blustery Atlantic wind, aggravated the retching. She became pale and felt bloated and tired.

The shape of the land on the horizon was sighted amid much joy! As many passengers as could be accommodated on deck were jostling for a position at the prow, hoping to be the first to view anything possible, of the new world. As the ship entered the New York Estuary and sailed towards Ellis Island, passengers were craning their necks forward, straining their eyes hoping to be the first to see the Statue of Liberty towering over the water between the two massive land masses of the estuary, shrouded by the morning mist. Shapes of city buildings could be made out indicating the already advanced development of New York.

The famous landmark had been built by Frédérick Auguste Bartholdi. It was a copy of his original statue in marble on Ile de France, an island in the Seine in the French capital of Paris. That statue celebrated the nation's freedom after the revolution. The giant copy was created in segments out of copper and was delivered in those pieces for assembly in situ on Ellis Island in 1875. The pieces were assembled between 1876 and 1882. It was then wonderful that the McCormicks were privileged to see it in its youth, not long after the assembly completion and the lifting of the lamp of liberty held aloft. The ship's foghorn blasted and other foghorns replied as shapes appeared and disappeared in the low-lying cloud hugging the water.

Finally, they berthed at the dock having arrived safely at last. Here disembarkation began. It was truly horrible! The travellers were herded hither and thither like cattle. From triumph to mayhem. Inhumanely men, women and children were sorted into separate corrals for medical checks, creating shouts of outrage from parents and miserable cries of fear from the children. The noise was deafening and the mood hostile.

In times past, sickness had been brought from distant lands and a system had been created at Ellis Island to examine every arrival's health. The Seventh Day Adventists managed the clinical side of the procedures. Infectious passengers were quarantined, or often turned back and sent to their port of origin. Frail people suffering simple hardships of the journey, or those who looked too undernourished and weak to be able to work, were sent to infirmaries for treatment. Pregnant Mary looked poorly and pale, and she and her children were directed to the infirmary. Little Lilian was incorrectly diagnosed with smallpox due to the presence of festering flea bites; and was sent away for isolation and treatment. Mary was beside herself as she heard the terrified wails of her little girl being led officiously away from her. Young Andrew was declared in good health and returned to his father.

Due to the crush of the infirmaries, it took a while for the doctors to realise that Mary was indeed in good health, merely pregnant. By then Lilian was also listed as well. However, a shocking administrative error resulted in her being labelled as an orphan and she was put up for adoption. Such was their welcome to the "promising and dreamed, of new life!"

## Chapter Five

## Rude Awakenings

*"And the mother gave, in tears and pain, the flowers she most did love; She knew she should find them all again in the fields of light above."*

*Longfellow – The Reaper*

Alexander and Andrew found Mary and the three of them began searching frantically for little Lilian in the muddled bureaucracy of the overworked medical and civil authorities. They had found a room to rent on the island, and day after day they returned to the authorities, reporting their missing child, telling everyone that would listen, that they would not budge until they knew the truth. Finally, after several weeks, they were directed to the Seventh-day Adventist administrative offices that kept records of infirmary admissions and releases; and worse still – adoptions! Their funds had by then begun to run low and general anxiety ran exceedingly high. They were finally informed that an error had labelled Lilian as an orphan and she had been adopted by a Seventh-Day Adventist family, which after many years of failing to conceive, had decided to search for a little child to adopt. They had fallen in love with pretty blue-eyed, titian-haired, bewildered and frightened; little Lilian.

Outraged by this error, Alexander and Mary who, torn between relief and fury had briefly collapsed, demanded the return of their child. A meeting was convened and the two families met. Lilian was not in the room, sheltered elsewhere with a nurse in attendance, to protect her from possible shock and trauma since she had already seemed, in the eyes of the authorities who had completed the documentation, to have settled quietly into her new family. Due to the nature of the meeting, another nurse entertained Andrew in a separate room. The two couples then argued over the situation. It was a torment of emotional strain. Both couples wanted "their daughter". Birth parents argued that the adoptive parents had no rights. The adoptive parents were citizens and had the law on their side, and seemed to have no concern for the anguished "foreign, impoverished peasant farmers" mother and father.

The crunch that broke Mary's heart was the realisation that this couple was wealthy and well-educated, and could offer Lilian so much more than she and Alexander could in the foreseeable short term. Here was an opportunity for her in a fine house in the green suburbs, and to attend a good school for young ladies, learn how to live a cultured life, and possibly marry well one day.

How does one sever the bond between parent and child, and of that between twins that had lain together in utero till birth, suckled together at the same breasts, and been raised till that time in a well-knit loving family? Oh, the heart-wrenching decision! To put the needs of others before your own desires, having no care for your personal loss, and laying your happiness on the sacrificial altar of choice.

This tragic event had a long-range impact on the members of the McCormick family. Finally, Mary and Alexander agreed that the wealthy New York couple could keep Lilian, but that they were to report from time to time on her progress. Being new immigrants, as yet unemployed, they needed to move on and start their new lives urgently. Mary would try to settle nearby and remain in contact until Alexander had permanent work and could offer them a home. Lilian was duly left in the care of the kind adoptive parents, members of the Seventh-Day Adventist community. Mr and Mrs Gerricke gave Mary and Alexander their address, and the two couples agreed to communicate by post once the McCormicks had settled.

That night the aftermath of recent weeks, and shock and heartbreak, caused poor sorrowful Mary to miscarry. Hollowed out and bleeding, emotionally and physically, Mary was pale and dull-eyed with shock. Doubled over with physical pain, loss and heartache she never spoke for several days but merely huddled on the bed in their rented room. Of necessity, Alexander went about searching for work of any kind but, with his little wide-eyed son trailing along, potential employers were reluctant to offer him anything.

After a while hunger and sorrow decreed that Mary should take action to find work for sanity's sake, in a domestic position that would provide address and accommodations, and hopefully a small stipend that could be saved. And Mary of the "lion-heart" did indeed do so! But it broke her spirit. In possession of the Gerricke's address, Mary went knocking on doors in the area looking for work as a governess or housekeeper. For days she went up and down among the grand houses until eventually, she found a position.

She entered a new social class that was not something she had ever expected. Before marriage, she had been a school teacher and pianist. She entered the life of a farmer's wife full of romanticised images of the picturesque existence on the land. She fed the chickens and collected eggs and tended the vegetable garden and the patch of flowers in the front of the house. She cleaned and polished and took time to sit at her piano which had moved in with her when they married. She had baked and cooked and embroidered and even painted from time to time.

Back in Glasgow, when she realised that she was pregnant she wandered around in a haze of bliss. Her new activities were the creation of little garments. After a few months, the local doctor told her that she was expecting twins and warned that she should take afternoon rest. Obediently she did so, although propping herself up on pillows, as she continued fashioning little garments. Alexander acquired two bassinets. That year was the first that the late arrival of summer did not thaw the land. The winter continued through April, May and June. During July there were occasional days of weak sunshine and in August it was briefly warmer and brighter. Then Autumn winds and chills arrived with a vengeance heralding in a frosty September. During that September the twins were born. For five successive years, the cold gripped Northern Europe, playing havoc with crops and livestock.

Now in New York, her employment was "below Stairs" as the scullery maid and her sleeping accommodation above stairs was in the attic eaves, where her view was of a variety of pitched roofs, chimney pots, weather vanes and cooing, strutting city pigeons. Occasionally she spied a stork's nest. Bereft of her family and coping with an unexpected change in social status, she retreated into herself. She worked diligently but was not participating in any kind of social awareness. She retreated into her drudgery. Her hands reddened and roughening made her weep. Back home there had been lanolin for her skin. Her only thoughts were of hope that Alexander would find land to work, or solid employment with which to earn enough to cover their new start together, and would quickly send for her.

## Chapter Six

## Pioneering

*"O traveller, stay thy weary feet; Drink of this fountain, pure and sweet; It flows for rich and poor the same. Then go thy way, remembering still, The wayside well beneath the hill, the cup of water in His name."*

*Longfellow – Inscription on the Shanklin Fountain.*

After many attempts to find casual gardening or building labour occupation, Alexander accepted failure in the immediate region where Mary and the Gerrickes were. He and his son Andrew started the itinerant life of migrant labourers. Whenever they could they wrote to Mary, at first via the Gerrickes, who afterwards informed them where she was employed. Thus, she always knew more or less where they were and what they were doing. Oftentimes they worked on the land through the harvesting season for a few weeks, elsewhere on land preparation and then in planting as the crop types and seasons changed. At that time much of the economy in America was agrarian and working the land was what Alexander understood.

A major economic boom resulted from the discovery of iron ore deposits and the creation of the Pittsburgh Steelworks. This was dangerous and hard work and not to be considered by a man with a young son in his care. Sometimes they only found daily employment. Other times they worked in one place for a week or two. On occasion, they mixed clay and laid bricks. For a time, they worked in a yard where there was carpentry being done for a large house. Here they held frames steady for the experts who filed and joined and nailed and smoothed with finer files. Consider the practical experience and educational opportunities this mixed work presented to young Andrew.

Many nights were spent sleeping under the stars sheltering against haystacks; on others, they settled in barns. Although they often slept rough, as casual labour, they were always fed at least once a day meaning that the frugal Scot, Alexander, was able to collect growing amounts of money in a leather pouch on his belt.

Fortunately, they arrived in the warm, moist climate of the tropical coast curving around the Caribbean sea, where there were Sugar plantations and Tobacco plantations. The warm weather was comfortable for sleeping rough, except for the occasional heavy downpour that steamed as it hit the ground.

Father and son, travelling as migrant labour, became a legend. Periodically, times were disappointingly, heartbreakingly difficult. This led to Pappa Alexander and his young son Andrew travelling over land doing odd jobs here and there as road workers, and even at times helping to lay railway lines. They did all kinds of work, both learning many skills fairly well if not perfectly. Alexander had a strong man's body, but his young son Andrew always his assistant where he worked, was still small yet developing a strong wiry frame through work. Not being able to work as well as his father and earn his own wage would diminish the young man's self-esteem and foster a sense of being less than whole in later years.

Travelling and working in this way, they experienced many beautiful and strange things on a new continent with wide-open spaces and clean air. The daily tasks provided a steep learning curve and inspired growth and increased courage in them both, as they regularly overcame unexpected challenges and proved that the impossible was indeed possible. Yet they yearned, yea ached, for Mary.

In her case, she was a subdued shadow of herself. She had given away her daughter, lost her unborn child, and no longer attracted respect as a wife and homemaker such as she had enjoyed no matter how humbly, in Scotland. She yearned for the purple heathered hills and wept at night for her husband, her son and her daughter. She wept over the hardships that life had dealt her. In her daily work, she merely bobbed a curtsey when receiving instruction, going about her duties quietly and sorrowfully. The other staff in the house teased her, calling her "Mary of the Sorrows". She could not feel as if she fitted in. When the other staff members joked and chuckled below the stairs, she had no smile. She never spoke of her family or her past. Nor did she confide in anyone about herself, during the conversations when the other women were more than loquacious on occasionally deeply personal topics.

Working wherever possible, Alexander and Andrew travelled South and then West, from sultry Florida to the wide-open spaces of Texas where ranches were enormous and there were vast corn plantations. There was a massive migrant populace and at times, the two found work in land preparation and reaping of corn. Occasionally in a rough hamlet, Andrew would feed and groom horses in livery while Alexander pulled pints in a bar. Moving South West, they encountered the barren scrublands of Mexico, where they came face to face with the Mayan temples that they had not known about, and marvelled at their ancient architecture.

There they found occasional work on a ranch. The desert country produced succulent plants with fruits they had not seen before. As they walked and worked here and there where rivers occasionally flooded, watering the surrounding plains, allowing for agriculture and beef, and even occasionally travelled on a post coach; they talked. Alexander took his paternal duties seriously, educating his son as best he could by engaging with local people to learn more about the land they were in; at other times he recounted stories from the Bible to Andrew, for the sake of instilling sound moral values in his son.

They plunged through the snake and mosquito-infested jungles of Panama all the while marvelling at the incredible birdlife above as they wound their way through the valleys, looking for ways to earn a living. Following the coastlands of Colombo which they found to be barren, they travelled East and South to plains laced with rivers where coffee trees abounded. Here they found work picking beans and later pruning trees. Then they migrated South, into a similar environment in Ecuador, where there were also coffee plantations as well as tea and tobacco lands. There were many signs of Inca history. By now, they were speaking respectable native Spanish.

They avoided the high mountains where farming if any was conducted on ancient Inca terracing. Accordingly, they veered around the mountains South Westwards, following a wide valley blessed with a strong flowing river which reputedly led to a lake. They camped and hunted and fished, and rested on the lake for some time, searching for wild fruits and vegetables, feasting on the hunted flesh.

From there it was possible to cross the lake and enter Chile which reputedly was keen to embrace European farmers. One glorious morning some native people arrived with a long dug-out canoe. They helped Alexander and Andrew to travel across the lovely still water, through the valley that leads to Chile and bade them farewell as they went off on their own business.

Imagine the exhilaration of the new scenery and wildlife-related dangers notwithstanding! They had lost all track of time as they had crossed deserts and plains and mountains and very briefly veered into Brazil's dense green jungle, covering hills and valleys flowing with many rivers, infested with alligators, and thick foliage, where there were enormous anacondas and mosquitoes breeding malaria.

Travelling South West attracted to the setting sun's rays that painted the skies gloriously, they eventually arrived in the beautiful wide-open spaces of the plains of Chile, bordered on the East by the great spine of the Andes, and to the west by the escarpment leading to the beautiful Pacific Ocean.

They had come a long way from looking for a new life farming the outskirts of New York to the wilds of Chile. Here there were many opportunities offered to farmers. Much agriculturally rich land lay awaiting development by those willing to work hard to prosper. All through the long weeks and many months of itinerant casual labour as they moved from one opportunity to another, and essentially living rough; Alexander had been carefully accumulating any cash that had not been used for survival. Working as casuals as they travelled South, they learned from others in the work teams, of Chile's history, natural mineral wealth, and many opportunities.

In Santiago Alexander was able to pin a claim for a small license, South of the small town of Los Angeles, in the undeveloped area towards Temuco in the region of Arauncania, a broad riverine plain. The river by that name is so called because of its reddish silt-carrying waters that wind through the Andes creating a natural pass where there is today a wide road for motorised traffic. His land claim was called Casilla and consisted of fifty hectares. Feeling a great sense of "arrival" after a long journey, Alexander purchased a tent and some bedding materials, a hoe, a pick, a shovel; and some copper cookware. These he loaded onto the backs of two mules as he and Andrew finally each had a mount. Together thus equipped, they continued Southwards.

"Back in the sixteenth century, these lands were occupied by the Indians Known as "Collunche" or "Cayunche", which in their native tongue means "dweller of the soft lands".

"Upon the arrival of the Spaniards, this place was soon called "Laia Island", as this is a sandy territory bordered by the Laja and the Bio-Bio Rivers. The conquerors built a large number of military forts to sustain the position of the white man in the region. It was not until the 18$^{th}$ century, that the then-governor of Chile, Don José Manso de Velasco, ordered the foundation of the village of Los Angeles.

This took place on March 20$^{th}$ 1739, under the command of Major Pedro de Cordova y Figueroa and the staff under his charge, who performed the first tasks, which included the location of the Main Square, the layout of the streets and the borders of the land plots to start building the first public institutions, such as the Church and what would later become the Town Hall.

Even if this was the key spot for the Spanish conquest, there were no settlements on these lands for a long time and the agricultural boom only took place a century later. But it was during the 20$^{th}$ century that the city changed as a result of the population increase in the capital of the Bio-Bio regions. Today development is evident. The peak of beef, dairy and agricultural activities has materialised in local industry and exports. Forestry activity is another big treasure in the area.

Bernardo O'Higgins was its most distinguished citizen. He stood out as the first mayor in 1810. On January 10$^{th}$, 1811, he was chosen by the people as a representative from La Laja (As this province was known in those days) for the First National Congress, a key institution where the spirit of national independence began to take place."

They had a long journey ahead to reach Casilla.

## Chapter Seven

## Casilla

*"The past and present here unite  
Beneath time's flowing tide,  
Like footprints hidden by a brook, but seen on either side."*

*Longfellow - A Gleam of Sunshine*

One can imagine the life of an erstwhile Glaswegian farmer accustomed to constant dampness, cold and pollution, who found himself and his young son in the wide-open, relatively undeveloped plains, lying between the Andes mountains and the escarpment which fell away to the great pale blue Pacific Ocean. Let your mind's eye roam wide grey-green grasslands hemmed by dense natural woodlands, bordered on one side by the beautiful sea coast just beyond the escarpment, and on the other by the Great Andes mountains where some of the world's highest and most challenging peaks for modern-day climbers are. There are many lakes, large rivers and several active volcanoes in the region. The freedom and the fresh air must have been heady and exhilarating. The land that they claimed lay some days' travel on difficult roads, towards Temuco. From there, they sent a telegram telling Mary that they had arrived in Chile and staked a claim just North of Temuco, called Casilla.

Heady freedom at last! Now they could build a home, create a farm and call for Mary. This thought energised them and they went to work with joy. It was a rough life involving hard effort and diligence. Where does one begin on a task of this size? Breaking virgin land and building a home, fencing sections for animal keeps, and finding a water source. Ultimately, they planned on developing a herd of beef cattle and sturdy working horses. In the immediate short-term they needed a home they could invite Mary to come to. It would be heavenly not to be camping anymore. Of vital importance, it was necessary to dig a well for water. And stake out sections of land in the immediate environs of the future dwelling.

For Alexander, it was hard work with only his young son as an assistant, even though young Andrew had grown in height and strength. The recent life they had been living, had toughened the boy, who was now older than his years through experience and travail. They enlisted the help of some local tribesmen. The friendly locals assured them that there was water underground and offered to help them build a home of sorts. While Alexander had some money stashed in his leather pouch, it was not much. He had to be careful how he shared it out.

While several of the welcoming neighbouring tribesmen assisted by cutting trees and dragging them to the site on rough, wooden trailers behind their sturdy horses, the others dug for water. Young Andrew learned to also drag young cut trees behind their newly purchased mules. Logs were sawn for building, and thatching grass was collected for raising up the small hut that was originally their plan for shelter.

Within several days, water was found! There was much celebration and joviality. Then the next arduous stage was the collection of suitable rocks to be dropped into the hole to prevent mud from welling upwards with the water, including suitable rocks and stones for the well's support wall. Then Alexander, experienced with this activity, climbed into the hole and built drywall reinforcement up the sides to secure the soil and prevent collapse. At one point, he needed young Andrew on his shoulders to complete the top layers under his instruction.

As a boy, he had done this with his father. Alexander was working in steadily rising water and one of his assistants had to rig and drop a skin bucket to lift out the water, pouring it away. The Amerindian tribesmen were conversant with this ancient method, as was Alexander, based on generations of experience in Scotland. Finally, it was done, and with water supply security, work began on the shelter. Even as they worked on the small rough dwelling, it was also necessary to pen the mules.

Of urgent concern to Alexander was how to reward the men that were helping him. The great journey from Scotland and their ultimate arrival in Chile had not provided many opportunities for more than personal upkeep. But his new neighbours were very kind and helped with energy and co-operation, from time to time offering well-needed advice. After several days of effort, the simple two-roomed wood-cut hut was built with a small hearth for heating and cooking, and a privy dug outside, enclosed with wooden slats for airing. The helpful neighbours had been very kind. It was agreed that he would offer them paid work as soon as he was able.

Several days later, he and young Andrew travelled with their mules to the growing village of Temuco, where there was a small banking institution. Based on his land claim that he had begun to develop, he was afforded a loan, the size of which terrified the frugal Scotsman on the one hand, but also enabled him on the other. Next to the bank was a post office and a newsagent. Alexander posted a letter to Mary to tell her they had arrived, staked a claim and were building a house and starting a farm. He described where they were and begged her to find a way to join them. He would never expect her to travel the hard way that he and young Andrew had. He suggested that she travel by sea to Buenos Aires, and then wait for him to fetch her. He had heard that the telegraph train from Buenos Aires travelled to and from Temuco and occasionally had a small car added for a few passengers.

They acquired more basic tools, vegetable and corn seeds, and a two-wheeled cart with suitable leathers and a yoke for the mules. Then they found a sturdy mare and stallion; and began the journey back, with the horses bridled, reined and tied together, and attached by rope to the cart; trotting along behind. The cart was regally pulled by the two mules appropriately dressed in leather rigging. Alexander and Andrew enjoyed that this time they were driving as passengers with their purchases. Victoriously they returned to the little claim and humble homestead. The horses and mules were turned out into the yard to graze and were offered water from a bucket. Because there was not yet fencing, they were hobbled. The fencing became a priority so Andrew was detailed to spend every second day felling suitable young saplings which could be used for fence poles.

Alexander and young Andrew broke the land that had never been worked before. They cleared out stubborn grass by the roots, and manfully dug out scrubby bushes, collected loose rocks, tossing them to the edges of the plotted-out land. Alexander had pegged its planned extent and marked it with rough hessian cords. Soon they were digging the land to loosen it, turning in the dried-out grass and leafy branches of the small bushes. All roots had been burned to prevent regrowth, and the plant material was chopped and returned to the soil for land enrichment. The heavy night dews and morning mists, as well as the occasional frontal rain that blew across the land from the West; ensured the breaking down of the rough compost and prepared the soil. And all the while Andrew worked on his first fencing task.

In the latter days of the cold season, they dug and ridged the soil, so that water was trapped between the ridges to soak into the land. Then as the days gradually lengthened, they sowed their seeds and prayed. At that point, Alexander involved himself in the fencing project with Andrew. The mules and horses were finally corralled. One bright sunny morning they saw young shoots above the soil and the two of them danced and shouted and gave thanks to the Lord their God.

One of the men that had helped them with the tree-cutting and log preparation and building of their hut, came to visit one day with his son Sandro, to see how they were progressing. Proudly Alexander showed his little crops to his old friend. He promised to trade some vegetables and corn in exchange for a young heifer and an adolescent bullock. He visualised ultimately allowing this heifer and bullock congress and thereby starting his livestock development. The men decided it was time to strengthen the fenced paddock for the horses and mules and to sort out a proper trough for water. The arrival of spring emboldened Alexander to travel again to Temuco, with young Andrew. This time they invited Sandro to come along for the adventure. Hitching up their little cart, they started the journey to town, proudly travelling in the cart behind the mules. What a treat!

Once there, Alexander decided to purchase some blankets, more tools, a kettle and coffee. He also bought two young fillies, as well as sacks of potatoes, onions, corn seed and a large bag of oat seed. At the post office, they found a letter from Mary saying that she had left her employment and had started her journey. She had savings to cover her costs. She had found out that it was indeed possible to travel from Buenos Aires to Temuco whence they could bring her to Casilla. She had heard that it was quite well-developed and had roads, small towns and villages. That there were rumours of railway travel as well as stagecoach travel. At this point, she was investigating the least expensive route from New York to Buenos Aires. Alexander replied that he would meet her anywhere she wished, he could not wait to see her again. They had proved that postal services were effective and they intended to remain in contact with the Gerrickes.

Back at the farm, Alexander and Andrew and occasionally Sandro, worked another patch of land and planted some oats, and created a potato patch and an onion patch. They prepared more land and planted the corn seeds. They kept what they had not planted for use at the table. In anticipation, they built a couple more rooms onto the house, with slatted wooden shutters to close the windows against bad weather. They built another room with a door to the garden including a huge hearth where simple cooking could be done indoors. It was deemed necessary to return to Temuco and acquire some bedlinen and kitchenware. They found a table and two benches and put them on the cart along with linen and some cookware.

In a frenzy of activity, hope and delighted anticipation, Alexander threw himself into homemaking for his wife. Sandro's mother, having heard of the impending arrival of Mary came to the house one day with some earth-baked terracotta cooking pots. These could be soaked in water and then placed in the coals for roasting of meat and vegetables. Her sister also came along one day, with a colourful woven mat for the floor. It was thick and rough and dyed with natural earthy pigments. Alexander was touched to the core of his soul by the generosity shown by these women towards his wife even before meeting her.

They also fed the stallion some oats and waited. In the interim Sandro and Andrew became fast friends. Andrew felt a certain lightening of the spirit in anticipation of his mother's arrival. The boys roamed the country surrounding the farm, playing hide and seek and other boyhood games. Further afield they climbed trees and explored the world around them. Alexander left the boys with Sandro's parents and travelled to Temuco to see if there might be news of Mary. There was none. Disappointed and anxious he returned, having acquired some chinaware plates, cups and saucers, a teapot, a milk jug and a sugar bowl. Sugar was available at great expense imported from the Caribbean islands, but could be found from time to time. Although he had heard that sugar plantations were now appearing in Venezuela which was nearer to hand. He also brought back some hens and a cockerel.

Wild Alpacas and Llamas were attracted to the young farm by the budding crops and the livestock. They were seen occasionally peering over the rough fences, so Andrew offered water and a vegetable for chewing from time to time. The natives encouraged these as they easily domesticated and their fur lends itself to spinning and weaving. Most of the "Amerindian" women knew how to comb out the thick rough fur and collect it for matting and twining before spinning.

With the arrival of spring, both the heifer and the two fillies gave birth. There was much rejoicing. Around the same time, the Llamas that had been visiting were encouraged to stay and came to live among the horses and cattle. Then one day an Alpaca with twins trotting behind her came and appeared to be asking for a home. They were welcomed in. On another occasion, Sandro's father brought his stallion to visit the mares. In exchange, he took Alexander's stallion to visit his mares. This was to protect both herds from harmful inbreeding. Around this time, Alexander was applying his mind to funding his starter beef herd with some dairy heifers.

One day a horseman arrived from Temuco bearing a telegram from Mary. She had arrived in Buenos Aires and was on her way to Chile via the Upsallata pass through the Andes. She had joined a group of people travelling this way, on the newly completed Transandine narrow gauge mail train, and their anticipated arrival was soon. The projected arrival date if all went well, crossing the pass and travelling through the new tunnel, would be in the next two days or so. The official postal/telegraph route was the one Mary had taken. And Temuco was the postal depot for the wider area!

## Chapter Eight

## Reunion in Chile

*"Whate'er my desire is, in thine eye may be seen.
I am King of the Household, And thou art its Queen."*

*Longfellow – Annie of Tharaw*

Alexander and Andrew put the small cart loaded with the tents and bedding behind the mules and took off in the direction of Temuco with joyful hearts. After a little less than a day's ride, they arrived in Temuco. The terrain was broken by many small rivers streaming off the mountain range, and the crystal-clear waters would provide for the brews of coffee. They had brought with them some cornmeal loaves, butter, hard-boiled eggs and wild berries for fruit.

They were waiting on the platform when the little mail train arrived. What a joyful reunion it was! What exclamations of delight and laughter and hugging of one another! A night's rest, refreshment and time spent enjoying the spectacular views ensued before they turned back and headed for Casilla.

This was the first time Mary had camped outdoors with her husband and son in their new land. Mary had happily brought some money with her, having not invested everything she had saved on her journey. Alexander posted a sign in the general store that he would like to purchase a small starter herd of cattle and that he was on Casilla Farm.

Mary lost no time in assimilating with the women of the tribe, to learn their ways of homemaking in this new environment. She mended shirts and darned socks and planted wildflowers that she collected in the forest, in beds near the house. Under her loving care, the chickens seemed happier, and egg production increased. She learned ways to bake with the cornflour and suggested to Alexander that rye and wheat should also be planted alongside the oats. Mary worked like a "whirling dervish". Her hands were always busy yet her moods were quiet and sombre. Her head was bowed and her expressions varied very little. Her presence in the house improved the living standards for her Husband and son but there was a dullness about her, an oppressive aura around her.

She seemed to have not brought with her the joy that Alexander was anticipating. Often when he looked into her eyes the absence of her old joy and good humour was chilling and of concern. At night he tried to cradle her in his arms but she stiffened and retreated to the edge of their bed refusing his advances. Wounded and confused by this rejection he did not try again. He tip-toed around her afraid of an anticipated eruption of subdued emotion. Between them there hovered the spectre of Lilian whose absence was keenly felt. Each of them avoided discussion for fear of the dam burst of emotion that seemed imminent. Andrew, ever sensitive to the incompleteness of the family spent more and more time outdoors with Sandro on boyish escapades.

One day Alexander raised the topic of Lilian. Had Mary given a forwarding address to the Gerrickes when she had left her erstwhile employers to travel to Chile? She had. Did she want to travel to Temuco to check for the post? She didn't. Deep in her heart, Mary had finally decided to bid her daughter farewell and to put an end to the sorrowing. She applied her mind to diligent concentration on the present time and to put her best foot forward.

Perpetually embarrassed by the fact that his lovely wife had been in service to accumulate savings and thereby be in contact with Lilian's new family. He understood the price she had paid to ensure her daughter's well-being; but as a man, he lacked the words to speak of these things. Then one day she suddenly asked him if he had ever wondered about the child that had been conceived just as they had left Scotland. Ashamed he hung his head and confessed that he had not even realised she had been with child.

She raged at him accusing him of being insensitive and self-oriented, unaware of her suffering and ordeals. How could he not have noticed how she had suffered from morning sickness during the journey? He had thought it was seasickness, not being aware of other personal signals of pregnancy. Shocked by these revelations he tried to take her in his arms to comfort her, but she stiffened and pulled away. Having allowed Lilian to go on with her newer, better life, Mary still struggled with the loss of the child she had not carried to term. She needed to vent her feelings and poor Alexander was the sounding board.

Andrew was struggling with a sense of displacement. He had grown accustomed to being his father's only companion, friend and working partner, with their relationship having been developed to that shared by two men, rather than of father and son; as they had travelled and worked to arrive where they were. Now that his mother enjoyed the full focus of his father's attention, he keenly felt the absence of his twin sister. In fact, he mourned the situation as it had developed, and his acute awareness of himself as no longer being a focus of attention with either parent, hurt deeply. His relationship with his father had become man-to-man, as opposed to father and son; and he was no longer young enough to attract the mothering he had hoped for.

He felt very much like a fish out of water, flapping around helplessly and with no sense of direction. The familial intimacy and fondness had been damaged and none of them could find a way back to the way that they fondly remembered it having been before.

Time passed and the vegetable plot grew rich and fertile and produced well. The oats also flourished, and the rye and wheat crops grew full heads as they bent in the breezes and changed from green to gold. Annually seeds were collected to plant a bigger spread of the grain. Thus, they had increasing grain to enrich the food of the animals. Alexander made the occasional trip to the market at Temuco, his cart loaded with potatoes and onions and other root crops for sale, along with bags of grain. Gradually he paid back his loan and became more or less self-sufficient. There was never a letter at the post office from the Gerrickes.

In silence Mary and Alexander closed the doors to their hearts and went through the motions of normal life, each aching within for the lost joys of Scotland. In their memories, the days were always bright and the air clear and sweet smelling. The farm they had sold had become a beautiful estate in their memories. Scotland the brave and fair became romanticised as a dream that they yearned for but had lost. Mary took to embroidering various linens with little blue and grey-green thistles. Her tartan shawl hung on a rail as an ornament in the living room. Homesickness is a painful illness.

As the seasons changed, Andrew and Sandro moved their growing herds back and forth, from the plains to the verdant valleys in the mountain range. There had been little attention paid to schooling though surely Alexander had taught his son some reading and reckoning and to balance the accounts from the farm, being the takings from the markets, and to cost out expenditures at the general dealer and ultimately regular payments against ownership of the claim. However, with the arrival of his mother, this was no longer his responsibility as it had been transferred to Mary in an effort to draw her into a sense of belonging in the new farm's development. The growing boy/man felt disenfranchised.

With the arrival of Mary, there had been some insistence on literacy. Accordingly, she and Andrew went to Temuco and there managed to find some books for sale in the post office. Some of these were in Spanish and one or two were in English. Andrew's bilingual education began and flourished from rough speech, gradually into something more genteel and poetic in style.

Andrew's companions from childhood had been Sandro and some of his village friends, dogs and chickens and goats. As growing boys approached manhood, they ranged the fields and forests and river valleys and lakes, in safe freedom. They developed a lifelong friendship as they roamed the countryside, possibly on horseback rambles. On all their youthful adventures exploring hills and plains and searching tunnels and chimneys in caves, squatting quietly next to waterholes full of wading Flamingos in their glorious pinks, and other exciting boyhood activities, they became adept with the use of simply made hunting bows and slingshots. Andrew became fluent in speaking Amerindian Indo-Spanish.

They roamed and explored the deep green natural forests. They hunted as young men do for birds of the air, robbed nests of eggs and on occasion trapped a silver-furred Andean fox or a small wildcat. High overhead huge Andean Condors flying with widespread wings, soared, swooped, circled, and glided on updraft air currents, then climbing dizzyingly and diving suddenly, wings folded back with talons stretched forward, as they too, were hunting small prey. They spied on and tracked Pudu, a small deer with shortish legs, reddish-brown fur and stubby, blunt-ended horns. From time to time, they encountered Rhea a largish earth-bound bird nesting on eggs, dug into an earthen basin of the warm earth, as is done in Africa by the Ostrich and in Australia by the Emu. It was always impossible to dislodge the fiercely protective sitting parent bird to steal a large egg.

In the verdant valleys of the low hills leading to the Andes escarpment, they spied on the shy Heumul, a large deer with a crown of antlers similar to those found in North America and Europe. In the highlands roamed Guanaco of the Cameliad family, similar to Llamas and Alpacas. They have a shaggy reddish coat and are pretty animals with sensitive twitchy noses, largish ears and long legs. They are browsers, nibbling on green leaves wherever accessible. Most exciting of all, was the thrilling sighting of the occasional Puma on a kill, when they were safe to observe, due to sated appetites.

Alexander encouraged them to explore, and also to camp out overnight, always warning them to be on their guard against Puma which is a big cat resembling an African Leopard but without spots, and large enough to consider attacking a human. However, they felt safe in the company of their horses and armed with bows and slingshots. With their simple bows, they were capable of killing small animals for the pot and would return to the rough homestead with skins for furnishings and occasional waterfowl for the pot.

In the twentieth and twenty-first centuries in Rhodesia, Andrew's descendants were entertained by fond stories told of his life and adventures in Chile and were encouraged to enjoy the wild country of Rhodesia and its natural inhabitants, by their Grandmother Winifred, one-time wife of Andrew.

On the odd occasion in summer, Alexander, Sandro and Andrew would travel far South to wander and camp on the Magellan coast, with its penguins and rocky fjords, and many islands offshore. The reason for this very short, well-timed visit was due to the Southern extremity of the continent being very cold, windy and stormy, even in Summer. At these times Mary was perfectly happy to have Sandro's mother in the house as a companion. They shared a lot about their ancestral backgrounds and customs and became firm friends. Mary never stopped grieving the loss of Lilian and the babe that had not gone to term, so she enjoyed the small children that accompanied Sandro's mother, who was given the name Piéta by a passing Spanish priest who had baptised her, when he had been evangelising the district around the time she was born.

Over time the farm in the Arauncania region of Chile began to flourish and Alexander used the manpower of his son and Sandro the faithful boyhood friend, more and more productively. They worked hard, branding their growing beef herd and then leading their cattle and horses to summer pastures in the hills and bringing them back again.

Together they added more rooms and a front porch to the log-built homestead. This involved cutting several trees and shaping the joints so that they fit at right angles. Thus, they spent a good amount of time in the forest, a little way off chopping and loading on the farm cart behind the sturdy mules and bringing them to the domestic area. The roof thatching was renewed as there was never a shortage of sturdy wild grasses. In a fever of domestic improvement, the yard area was greatly enlarged and the fence and gate were renewed. Also, they built a sizeable protective lean-to for the horses and a large barn for the cattle to shelter in during bad weather.

Alexander applied his mind next to the acquisition of land implements, as well as a team of cart horses, to draw the contraption. He knew it could be bought in segments and assembled. Off he went to Temuco and managed to purchase this long dreamed of wonder. They broke and cleared more land to plough and continued to plant and harvest oats, rye and wheat and American Corn in increasing quantities, on more and more of the land for animal feed, for sale and as well as for human rations. They even toyed with the idea of starting tobacco production. The odd steer was killed and salted for beef and in the area of the homestead, there was a kitchen garden patch that increased in size and variety of crops producing leaf and root vegetables for the table. Naturally, there was plenty of milk to be had though primarily these were beef cattle, not dairy herds. Chickens continued to be raised; thus, there were always enough eggs and regular roasted birds. Occasionally, Sandro ground the summer-dried maize into flour, and a coarse but delicious loaf was baked.

## Chapter Nine
## World at War

*"Take them, O Great Eternity! Our little life is but a gust,*
*That bends the branches of thy tree,*
*And trails its blossoms in the dust!'*

*Longfellow - Suspira*

It is so sad that the world erupts from time to time into fighting, causing so much disruption and death. The war that interrupted the lives of an entire generation, had been brewing for a long while and began to spark in sporadic parts of Europe. However much some individuals in the story might have been seeking glory and adventure, for others it meant disaster and horror. It was once said that there are regular wars or plagues designed to control the earth's population.

Years pass and boys grow into men. Having finally become an equal partner with his parents in the running of the farm, Andrew felt more at home; though his mother still seemed a little distant and sulky. But he enjoyed spending evenings sitting on the porch with his father watching the changing colours above and discussing the stars of the Southern Hemisphere. They sipped on homemade berry wine and relaxed after an arduous day's work. They had become comfortable companions and Andrew had begun to feel that he had grown into his physical size. From time to time, they quietly wondered between themselves, trying not to let Mary overhear, what might have become of Lilian.

The cropping lands grew in size and fertility and the dairy/beef herd grew. Occasionally they drove steers into Temuco for the sales and returned with little home comforts to try and make Mary happier. They dreamed of one day getting her a pianola. There were distant rumbles of war. The building of the Panama Canal, and its opening for business, had facilitated the sea path to much-increased shipping and fostered railway developments. More and more world news dribbled in.

There began to be increasing talk of war. It was a low rumble at first where men gathered on corners and whispered. Then when farmers gathered in Temuco at sales, they did not talk in whispers. They believed that their task was to stay on the land and increase their activities to be able to supply from Chile, the foodstuffs that would become unavailable in Europe when the war broke out.

At the age of thirty-six years, a restless Andrew Young McCormick responded to news of the Great War and the need for the services of men below the age of forty years who were fit and able and of British descent, and he became determined to enlist to fight. A deep-seated need to prove himself a man of valour and substance was behind this decision. He joined up with groups of his compatriots as they travelled North, at first overland, and then by sea across to North America, travelling on fishing skips from island to island in the beautiful Caribbean Sea. Landed in Miami, they continued North overland by rail to Manhattan where they set sail on a cargo vessel working their passage as they travelled. Dreaming of glory, the men were cheerful and full of courage and bravado as they sailed towards a greatly troubled European stage in the terrible arena that had been brewing and finally broke out in 1914. Arriving in Liverpool they found a war office and enlisted in the early months of 1915. After brief but thorough training in handling arms and general military discipline, he and others of his intake, being overseas volunteers were assigned to the Volunteer Corps and were sent to Europe. They crossed the channel to Bruges in Belgium and after camp training and briefing, the men were sent to Verdun as cavalry corps. Andrew was among these. They travelled with their company, dividing into regiments under their Officers and dispersed to various theatres of war.

Sandro had stayed behind on the farm with Alexander. And Andrew felt a sense of great emptiness without the constant companionship of his lifelong friend. But he soon learned to cooperate in his battalion and began to trust his Lieutenant. The original sense of adventure became a daily ordeal as war presented itself a grim reality of dodging fire, and surviving horrifying explosions as men lay face down to avoid too much injury. In the Battle of Ypres, men crawled overland in grim, wet and cold conditions, from one outpost to another. Often, they came under fire and had to return fire. Men on both sides were lost, hastily buried after their tags were retrieved, before all parties fled the scene, young men terrified by war. Andrew was miserable. He had dreamed of a kind of Napoleonic glory. But perhaps it had been this terrible then too. Andrew's ability to work with horses was discovered and he was transferred from his infantry regiment to the Cavalry Volunteers.

Boldly they crossed the river Verdun into a battle that was waged for many months in difficult circumstances. One cannot know anything of Andrew's ordeals, though we do know how terrible that war was. The Battle of Verdun in Northern France during 1916, vies for glory with the battle of the Somme. Although both these battles lasted very long and thousands died on both sides, the battle of the Somme ended up more famous, yet one cannot assume that the battle of Verdun was a lesser one. It was a hard battle with huge losses.

Andrew was a man on the cusp of middle-year maturity and yet was an unfulfilled boy at heart striving to prove himself. As a lover of horses and experienced rider and handler of horse and cart, it is possible that his heart broke, again and again, being part of a team or teams of men and horses dragging cannons up disgusting muddy hills in frigid wet weather. The men's boots and horses' hooves sucked into the black mud as they slithered and laboured, heavily laden with war kits, battle packs and weaponry. It could have been absolute torture seeing delicately bred riding and carriage horses being used as canon drays, overloaded and overworked, broken by their exertions and being put down there and then by a rifle-bearing soldier lacking the knowledge and finesse of a general veterinarian at the races.

Occasionally they were able to commandeer great heavy-work farm horses, but even then, the work they were given was overly arduous. One can imagine Andrew pulling at the loads to assist the horses he was so fond of. He was undoubtedly also exposed to terrible human death and destruction in the trenches. He was fortunate to enter the war late enough to have been issued with a gas mask as well as a tin hat.

By terrifying mischance, he was captured by the enemy and held under guard, with several others, in an abandoned farmhouse. Suffering his fear of execution in silence, he watched and waited and hoped and prayed, before one night seeing an opportunity to escape. Quick as a flash, he overpowered the inattentive, sleeping sentry, and was off and away as fast as he could run, without a sound, into the night. Yet even that escape was achieved in a manner that left him grieved and ashamed of what he had had to do to be free. Men do not tell their women how terrible their war experiences were.

He hardly dared twitch for fear of being seen, but move he must, to be away from whence he had scarpered. Keeping in the thickly forested land and always moving, hiding in snowy ditches, he was living from hand to mouth, and only moving at night. His wild years in Chile enabled him to survive on the run. But in Chile, he was never being hunted in winter snows and possibly by sniffer dogs. His fear was extreme. His nerves were constantly on the alert, his eyes searching ever around for opportunities.

## Chapter Ten

## Escapee

*"Naught avails the imploring gesture*
*Nought avails the cry of pain!*
*When I touch the flying vesture*
*'Tis the grey robe of the rain."*

*Longfellow – The Bridge of Cloud*

One early morning, Andrew was fortunate to observe a farmer's wife hanging washing on the line. He kept still and waited, watching the clothes flapping in the breeze to dry in the weak sunshine.

Then he saw her gather up her dog on a lead and with a basket on her arm walk briskly away from the house. He could not believe his good luck! Crouching low as he ran, he reached the line and fumbling in haste, stole the poor peasant's clothing. He was terrified. He had no idea whether the clothes were of a husband at work on the farm, sleeping in the house, or the same husband sent away to war. But he rationalised that older farmers might be exempt from service being needed on the land. He dashed into his hiding spot, bundled the clothes under his arm and fled deeper into the thick trees. He spread his treasure out on the forest ferns to dry in patches of sun, as they filtered through the trees. Keeping his substantial warm flannel British underwear, he buried the rest of his uniform and donned his new identity as a local land worker. But he knew he needed a woollen cap and scarf to complete his image and also a good, if worn-out, jacket. He wondered why he had not taken the opportunity to burgle the house where he had stolen the clothes, but there was no going back.

With this need in front of his mind, he was acutely aware of his surroundings as he felt freer to move in the daylight. He came across a railway line and, having become aware of another village in the distance, he followed the tracks. Sure enough, he saw a little station house ahead and approached among foliage on the opposite side of the track, to see what it consisted of. A few people were waiting for the train. These were older countryfolk civilians. Some had sacks tied with string as baggage and one man was travelling with battered and scratched leather luggage. Andrew retreated a bit and then quietly crossed the tracks and approached the station house on the other side of the line creeping around to approach from the entrance unobserved from the platform. Hidden in the shadows, he quietly watched the cluster of people. They appeared to all be familiar with one another although not specifically travelling together.

Andrew hovered, moving silently towards the group, assessing the situation. Then his luck arrived. The station master went out to inform the waiting people that the train was delayed. There was some grumbling about the indignity and discomfort of wartime. The conversation was that of tired people who could simply, no longer tolerate the growing inconvenience of war and invasion, and general disruption to their lives. Quietly, moving like a cat, Andrew slipped into the stationmaster's office and relieved it of the worthy gentleman's day jacket and plaid woollen cap with matching scarf. He slipped away unnoticed and after ten minutes of darting here and there in an attempt not to leave a trail, he paused, donned the stolen items, and strolled casually into the village as if he was a resident.

Now that he was no longer hiding in the forests, he was most alert to find an opportunity to enjoy a good warm meal. This was not an easy task in wartime France. People were enduring a system of rationing and used coupons to buy their food. Nobody bought more than they needed. As he came into the countryside again, he was alert to the possibility of smelling the aroma of baking or stewing or even the frying of eggs. Daylight wandering was too dangerous.

He slipped away from the road and headed for the safety of trees and scrubland. Then he heard water and followed the sound. There was a stream babbling along in a pretty green wooded area. Hidden close to his body was his British army-issue combat knife. He brought it to hand in case an opportunity came to kill for food. Ever alert, his eyes lit on a wild goose, her gander and their goslings, looking for an evening nesting spot. A tenderness in him prevented him from tackling that little feathered family. But as he paused and watched them, he saw a common fox slowly following them, ears forward, nose twitching and outstretched tail. Without any prevarication, he flung himself on the surprised canine and killed it with one stab between the ribs, as he and Sandro had been wont to do in Chile when out adventuring. The geese startled and made much squawking and honking as they flapped their wings, rising above the water's surface, herding their little goslings into safety away from this crazy human who had saved them from a stalking fox.

A good dinner later and a stretched fox fur around his neck for warmth, Andrew contemplated returning to Chile. As an escapee and deserter, he did not want to encounter a military base of any nationality and be questioned. At this point in time, he was mainly pleased that he had escaped recapture and survived this far. Having done that, he had the leisure to consider and admit to himself, that he was not made for heroics.

He wanted desperately to be home in Chile by whatever means possible. He managed to increase his disguise by picking up an unattended hoe in passing.

Eventually, he made good his escape, travelling as an unidentifiable labourer, across country fields and battle-scarred farms, and partially demolished villages, travelling ever West; setting his sight on landmarks in the late afternoon sun, he made his way at night through France. He realised that he could not return to Britain as he was a deserting soldier.

In a Café, hoping for some bread and wine he encountered some members of the French resistance. He was directed to a shepherd's hut on the French ascent of the Pyrenees, where a scout was known to lead groups at night, moving only in the dark and hiding by day, over the mountains into Spain, ultimately delivering them to an undisclosed office, where an undercover person provided them with travel documents and false identities.
He was more relieved than he could ever recall being when he encountered the scout and was accepted for the next "escape".

After two weeks of hiding out in the foothills of the Pyrenees waiting for a scout to fetch him, His chance came. He had been fed by local people, all of whom never used names. They appeared at night under the cloak of darkness, helped in whatever way necessary, and then disappeared again.

His chance came and he joined the group. They were silent. There was no exchange of names or background histories. They were unidentified souls that moved silently in the night following the guide. He never waited for them. It was up to them to keep him in sight and follow. There was an occasional hut where bread and coffee were found waiting for them. They never knew the identities of the people who helped them. The ascent and descent in the dark were perilous but they had to trust and keep the dark shape of the guide in sight to follow. It was left to each person to ensure their own safety.

Arriving in Spain he received his false papers and boarded a fishing boat, working his way on similar small vessels from village port to village port, and then in the Cape Verde islands, he managed to board another cargo vessel, this time travelling in a convoy. He eventually arrived in America near the Panama Canal, thirty-nine years old, shell-shocked and aimlessly wondering where to go and what to do next.

As he had as a child with his father, he worked his way across the land, travelling always South, as a day labourer, for food and lodging. Wizened, thin and ragged, he finally arrived back at the farm where he had grown up. There he was delighted to find both parents still in residence. They also seemed more relaxed than he remembered them being before he left. They had settled back into an appearance of marital peace and harmony.

It was wonderful to be part of a family again with his much more cheerful mother, spending time in the evening chatting with his father, the two of them sharing stories of the farm during the time in which they had been so sadly separated. They reminisced on life in Scotland. Mary cooked and sewed and baked. She had spun yarn and was knitting a warm jacket for Alexander. Andrew did not speak of his war experiences, merely encouraging his father to speak of the farm and local affairs. The horrors were too painful to reach and describe, and the manner of his return a matter of shame that he simply could not discuss. His father most wisely did not probe and Mary, immersed in comfortable domesticity had no interest in war.

Andrew was now a battle-scarred man in psyche if not in body. After a few weeks, he began to feel like an "extra", a person who was bent out of shape and could no longer fit in. He was jealous individually of his parent's relationship with one another and felt excluded from their comfortable companionship. He was desperate for attention from both of them. After a few weeks, he realised that a man of his age needed to strike out on his own. He heard that his vaguely remembered sister was also all grown and living in California and married. He knew that he would never be welcome in her life if he went to go and find her. Too much water had flowed under the bridge. He grappled with his sense of loss and loneliness.

Andrew sought out Sandro who invited him to mingle with the tribe while he considered his next move. They welcomed him as a brother, plied him with food and clothing, and friendly companionship as always. Yet even there he began to feel like he was not where he should be. The country beyond the high Andes was calling him. During his travels back to the Americas he had heard much talk of the amazing developments in Buenos Aires and how many people from Europe and the British Isles had gone there to make their fortunes in the years when war had been brewing. He needed a change.

A man of his age and experience was surely able to begin a new life.

## Chapter Eleven
## Adventuring in the Andes

*"When I compare what I have lost with what I have gained,*
*What I have missed, with what attained,*
*Little room do I find for pride."*

*Longfellow – Loss and Gain*

After several days of deep thought and tobacco chewing during which time Sandro tried to get him to talk his thoughts out of himself; Andrew suddenly suggested that they could go off adventuring over the Andes into Argentina. As yet unmarried and never one to miss an adventure, Sandro was quick to bid his family farewell, and they began travel preparations. They rounded up some riding horses and a couple of pack mules, loaded them up with bedrolls and thick woven overcoats, courtesy of Sandro's mother, aunts and sisters, and prepared to trek into the Andes, to experience an excitingly wild, adventure.

Although they planned to follow the general route of the Upsallata pass above the rail line, they agreed to try and remain in the wilderness surrounding the pass enjoying the wild and beautiful country. They would be camping among the mountain peaks and valleys, viewing glaciers and going to taste the fabled exotic world of Argentina!

News had been trickling through that Argentina was attracting adventurous men. Immigrants were pouring into the country from South Africa after the Boer wars, and vast ranches were opening up. Farmers were drilling windmill-powered wells, and in Patagonia occasionally struck oil. These were exciting times!

The early days and weeks were a general repetition of their boyhood adventures, exploring, hunting, and camping out. The weather was mild at first. They paused often, looking back to view the country they had already crossed. The freedom and fresh air were exhilarating. A big, thick-furred hound from Sandro's family village had come along. He was called Pronto, always bouncing around in loose-limbed excitement at being among his people, and now going on more than a couple of days of travel.

This meant that their ration hunting needed to cover three appetites. Pronto was an excellent retriever, always returning with birds that had been downed by Andrew or Sandro, or even rousing quails and other small animals not noticed by the men. In this regard, he was a real asset. With his great paws, slobbery smile, starry eyes, and alert but floppy ears, Pronto was a cheerful companion, to have along.

Gradually they reached the forested foothills and found the morning mists swirling in the trees. The early sunbeams pierced the shadows of the branches and danced between the leaves that were gradually changing colour, and drifting down to carpet the forest floor, as Autumn approached. The dancing sun rays, spotlighting occasional ground cover growth, were beautiful beyond belief.

Early one morning, after a night spent in the warmth and protection of the trees, camping against some sheltering granite outcrops, the two were woken by frantic barking and yelping from Pronto. The hobbled horses and mules were restless and whinnying. The men leapt up to investigate and startled some horse thieves trying to untie the hobbling amid the kicking of the horses. There was a brief scuffle between the campers and the thieves before peace was restored after the delivery of a couple of well-placed fists, and the retreating steps crunched on dry forest floor leaf cover. They realised that they ought to be more alert while travelling and setting up camp. Fortunately, they had lost nothing but their peace of mind and maybe a little innocence.

That day after breaking camp, they broke out of tree cover and started a gentle climb into the foothills of the mountains, more or less following the given directions towards the pass as decided. After the sun had risen and cleared the morning mist, they searched for a riverine valley that might lead them around the mountain towards the pass. From there they reasoned they would be able to view the deep Upsallata valley and famed river, as they climbed into the lower reaches of the range. Gradually increasing altitude, good sense warned them to not climb too high too fast. Sandro knew of altitude sickness and Andrew had the experience of his Pyrenees escape. They stopped on a level crest to allow the horses to graze, and Andrew kept watch while Sandro went hunting with Pronto.

This became a daily routine as the men alternated watching and hunting. In the evening with a kill slung on the back of one of the mules, they continued, looking for a camp for the night. Gradually they became aware of distant sounds, of roaring water, and followed the sound of the cascade. A bend in the hill exposed a heavily plunging waterfall. Careful inspection showed that behind the sheet of water, there was a cave that might be accessible. Andrew went ahead with his bow taut and ready to shoot in case he disturbed a resident human or animal that might pose a threat.

The cave was empty! After watering the horses and filling their canteens, they led the reluctant horses and mules into the shelter of the cave. There as darkness fell, they lit a fire and cooked their day's kill. That night, feeling safe hidden behind the cascade, they slept well.

The following morning as they emerged into bright sunshine, they searched for a suitable path to travel with the horses on the level from which the water tumbled. The horses and mules had to be led that day but their objective was achieved, and another night was spent near the water source, sheltering under a large wild fig tree. The two men decided to take turns watching during the night since seemingly these mountains were used by thieves, possibly moving a lot more than horses between Chile and Argentina.

In the morning, thick mist and a darkening sky promised rain. They travelled on a fairly level plain searching for shelter should there be heavy rainfall. Luck was with them as they encountered a herder's hut. The hut had a lean-to for the animals and a fire grate. A small stream trickled down some rocks due to heavier rain at a higher altitude. Kindling was collected and a few logs were added to the fire. Andrew returned from his sortie with a pair of plump waterfowl.

They sheltered there for several days until the sunshine returned. The clear view and bright sky revealed snow-covered peaks in the distance. Acknowledging that these might need to be crossed, they spent time hunting and fishing at every opportunity as they trekked ever upwards and onwards into the mountains, searching for a river-worn pass. As long as the weather was fair, they made good progress. But they both suspected that tough days lay ahead and they should find a trail not involving higher and steeper altitudes. This was no longer a simple boyhood adventure.

One morning as they lazily travelled enjoying the sight of the deep sky across which fleecy clouds were chasing one another, they rounded a bend to be confronted with a fully racked Heumel, - Andean deer. As quick as a shot Sandro unleashed his sling and stunned the deer. Almost at once, Andrew released his bow and the Heumal stopped kicking as he had been pierced at the jugular vein. This was a huge spot of luck. The two men spent the day skinning the rapidly cooling animal and pinned the skin on the ground to stretch and dry. As quickly as they could they quartered the carcass into sections and, after digging a hole for the fire, placed tree branches across the top, rubbed salt into the meat, and wrapped the portions in damp cloths for the process of curing.

This exercise meant that they had to stay there for a few days before moving on, so they set up camp. The horses were allowed to roam on long hobbles attached to another loose rope, as there was good grazing available and trees for shade. The men made a lean-to with tree branches and the drying Heumel skin, for their shelter. Once more they took turns keeping watch during the night.

Several days later they broke camp and moved on. Aware of the deepening autumnal weather, they eagerly scanned the mountains ahead for a good downhill passage into a protected valley between the looming snow-clad peaks. There was no way that they could take the horses through the high peaks and over permafrost and glacial land. A lower route between the peaks needed to be found. As they picked their way carefully down through a narrow valley, they encountered a group of travellers heading towards Chile from Argentina.

These were Chilean Amerindian men leading a good number of horses with them. What luck! They paused and shared some food and talked. The newcomers did not reveal much about themselves but were kind and open about the route they had taken from Argentinian La Pampa which they said was drained by several good rivers and was an easy travelling country from which they had arrived to this point.

They had travelled to Argentina, so they said, to trade and were returning with more horses which were a little more finely bred than their wild Indian steeds. They could direct Sandro and Andrew towards a good route that would be less taxing on them and their horses.

Pronto had growled quietly in his throat when the strangers arrived and hovered close to his master keeping a watchful eye on the strangers. Sandro took this as a warning and motioned to Andrew that they should bid the newcomers farewell and move on. Later he told Andrew that he knew of the steady horse trade between Argentina and Chile and that these men were likely horse thieves.

Thus, our two friends travelled at a fair pace towards the darkening East, to put some distance between them and the others. Thus, they never went further north in search of Upsallata. They reasoned that in any case, they had probably missed it.

Eventually, the evening sky and rising mist meant that they had to camp, and they again planned to take turns keeping watch through the night. It was a long and tense night but morning came with a golden glowing mist swirling around, and they broke camp and moved on before stopping to take refreshment. Having shared a goodly portion of their salted deer, rations were diminishing. There were still bones for Pronto.

Leaving Andrew on guard, Sandro and Pronto went off on a hunt. As the sky turned from gold to blue and the mist rose becoming high thin clouds, Sandro returned with a Pudu slung over his shoulders. This was good news. They quickly skinned it and butchered the meat, immediately getting some into a pot on a fire, to cook for immediate needs. The rest they treated with herbs and salt and hung out to dry. They planned to stay there and move on in the morning with their jerky and another skin added to their collection.

Days passed as they travelled East over terrain that was not always easy but which seemed to be a well-worn trail. Gradually they descended and began to leave the mountains behind them. Forested country approached and they looked forward to being able to forage for food among the trees. Here they found foxes and an occasional boar. Food became more plentiful and the temperatures easier to manage. There were streams for fishing and life was worth living.

From time to time, they met other travellers, as they descended towards the plains of La Pampa, and in the company of another group of travelling men, they helped one another to survive icy-cold windy temperatures during dark but starry nights. They huddled around campfires cooking their day's hunt and brewing herb teas or bone soups. These were groups of South Africans who after having arrived in Argentina, could not endure the constant wind on Argentinian plains and were, as a result, travelling to Chile.

The sharing of life histories was surely far more entertaining than hours spent slouched in front of modern-day television, simply passing time before falling into an overstimulated restless sleep. Thus, Andrew learned a bit about Southern Africa and its environment. The two sets of travellers separated heading West and East, the South Africans wisely choosing to cross the mountain range in Spring.

Imagine the young men in the spring, frolicking in waterfalls and lakes, cleansing themselves, and gathering wild berries for sweetmeats. Gradually, our pals made their way on the Argentinian plains, scruffy and bearded with long untended hair. Forests had given way to scrubland and eventually grasslands. Sandro instinctively knew as always before, where to find edible roots and crunchy leaves and herbs that kept them healthy. They had encountered Puma and Condors, snakes and giant lizards and deer and Alpacas in the wild. Countless birds inhabit the mountain foothills. Who knows how long it had taken them to pick their way through?

Not having tired of their adventure, they journeyed East enjoying the constantly changing views and the outdoor living in the wild. Ever and anon, they continued as before seeking adventure. At the odd outpost, they enjoyed the company of the people they met and made use of village square public pumps to wash, and water their animals. The horses and mules needed shoeing and after a search, they found a blacksmith who was happy to accept skins for the favour.

As they descended into the lush lower lands, leaving the La Pampa plains behind them, Andrew and Sandro veered north to avoid the mountain range looming south East of them. They had been travelling for several months now and were at this point, beginning to consider stopping somewhere for a while, to do some gainful work. As they travelled, veering North East, they heard of the great city of Buenos Aires on the edge of the sea where there was a vast bay from which you could look across on a clear day and view in the distance, the coast of Uruguay.

One day as they entered a small hamlet, they found an advertisement placed at the post office by the Cordner family which was ranching in the region of La Matanza, South West of the city of Buenos Aires. La Matanza means "Place of Great Bloodshed", remembering the many battles that had occurred there during the Spanish "invasion" and traumas of colonisation between the conquistadors and the native peoples. The wealthy Cordner family owned a large operation on which ranged an impressive herd of excellent beef cattle, and where they bred sturdy Clydesdale horses and sheep. The ranch required the extra hands of a cowboy or two. Manpower had become short with the rapid growth of operations in the region. So off they went, following vocal directions in search of it. Many people knew of the fabled farm and the wonderful Cordner family living there.

## Chapter Twelve
## Admirable Alan

*"But who shall dare, to measure loss and gain in this wise?*
*Defeat may be victory, in disguise.*
*The lowest ebb is the turn of the tide."*

*Longfellow – Loss and Gain*

According to Alan; Rhodesia had been populated by the second sons of the British aristocracy. The inheritors of the titles and the land went into the House of Lords in Parliament, spent the season in London, and the rest of the year in the country entertaining one another and riding out on the hunt. The second son went into business in the colonies. Solveig writes from hearsay only. This was his explanation for the "upper crust" behaviour of the English Rhodesians some of whom claimed to be of the aristocratic class.

After Alan bought his farm, one ever so "posh" farmer's wife informed him that, as a land owner, he had joined the aristocracy. Antics at the country club and at Polo meets supported this ideation. There had also at one time been an organisation known as the British South Africa Police, made up of elements of the South African British Colonial society, and some adventuring types from England who enlisted. These were a uniformed force that performed a sort of peacekeeping element in the country areas, where from time to time, trouble erupted between the local tribes and the farming society who lived a fairly comfortable life after the fashion of the British aristocracy.

Many years later when Solveig was living and working in Cape Town, she met through her business activities, a most gracious and interesting English gentleman named David Bullock. He had known Alan's father, whom you will meet as Ivor the Driver, from the gliding club in Salisbury when he had been in the B.S.A.P. He had also been a member of the Gliding Club and had on occasions been towed into an updraft by Ivor. He hailed from Stratford on Avon and was a repertory player in Shakespeare. A delightful and most erudite dinner companion he had been on a couple of occasions! But we digress, back to Alan.

We already learned of some of his childhood antics. He and his siblings and neighbourhood friends grew up in a wonderful safe social environment on large properties where there was plenty of space to run around on and hide in, trees to climb, and the huge undeveloped land behind the houses on the street, that was called the "vlei" (an Afrikaans word indicating low-level waterlogged land) for adventuring in. This land was dry and hard, covered in tall grass during the long sun-baked, dry winter; but that became waterlogged, sticky clay during the rains, and was considered not good for building on because of expansion and shrinkage in volume.

They attended the local schools. The co-ed Highlands Junior was followed by enrolment at the newly opened St John's Primary for boys, which in turn gave way to Oriel Boys High. In Hugh's case, it was Churchill. His sisters moved from Highlands School to Oriel Girls High School. In Rhodesia, the British Cambridge Education was and is still taught, and Cambridge O and A Level Examinations, are still written to this day. Cambridge University requires thirteen years of schooling for a university entrance.

However, in South Africa, there is a twelve-year system ending with a Matriculation Certificate, (reputedly equivalent to French Baccalaureat) which enables acceptance for tertiary qualification depending on the subjects chosen by the students. Children could thus leave school after the first of the two A-Level years, and be certified for M Level which was accepted as a matric.

Alan and his older brother Hugh completed their time at their boy's High Schools with M Levels and both having excellent abilities in Mathematics and technical skills, gained appointments in Government departments. Hugh joined the air force in the helicopter corps as a trainee flight engineer. Alan entered the Ministry of Works as a trainee Quantity Surveyor.

Later their two sisters in turn travelled to Cape Town and studied at the University of Cape Town on the slopes of Devil's Peak overlooking the city. Erica majored in Economic Sciences, afterwards studying further at Carnegie Mellon, a private research university based in Pittsburgh, Pennsylvania. Its predecessor was established in 1900 by Andrew Carnegie as the "Carnegie Technical Schools" in America. Tamsin studied Geology which she then continued with to the Ph.D level, in Boulder, Colorado.

Apropos Carnegie Mellon University, the narrator has learned that Andrew Carnegie of Scots descent, was a leading steel magnate in the $19^{th}$ century who became one of the richest men in America. He then was a well-known and revered philanthropist in America, Great Britain and the British Empire.

At the Ministry of Works, in a building fondly known as The Stables, situated next to the Parliament building, we find Alan as he continued working through his Technical Level Certifications, eventually achieving Level four qualification. By then, Rhodesia was experiencing her troubles and all the young men were in part-time military peacekeeping service. Alan served in "Air Supply". He hated this because he was always to be in the tail of the craft, having to toss out supplies as the plane did a low pass. This resulted in him being always green at the gills with airsickness from the "bouncing tail" of the craft.

Then he struck gold when his Minister in Charge at work, selected him as a supported part-time student at Durban University which also had a technical side called Howard College. Said University was on the hill near to where he had shared "digs" and where he had ridden past Solveig, as she walked from the bus stop to her family home of an evening.

He loved then and still does now, the sultry warm climate of Durban, swimming in the sea and most of all, weekend dashes up to St Lucia on the North Coast where there was a famous Rhino rescue park into which the Rangers were also introducing other wildlife. Alan was and is still highly intelligent and quick to understand concepts. His degree work at Howard College on Berea Ridge was a bit of a "walk in the park". He gained vast experience working for Mr Slater and as we know, also built himself an Austin Healey.

As stated, he has a very perceptive ability. At the time in Durban, there were several houses on a ridge sheltering Durban Harbour, known as "The Bluff", that simply fell into sinkholes as a result of having been built on unstable soil.

He applied his creativity to this, visiting the sites where the homes had collapsed and, examining the soil types and general geological structure of the whole ridge jutting into the sea, which created a buffer for the harbour. In his final year, he wrote a thesis on the subject, in which he described possible solutions through different styles of foundations. At that stage, Solveig was around and he proudly showed his work to her.

He was even happier when his book was judged so excellently, that it became required reading for all students of related structural degrees. She was incredibly impressed since he had never seemed to be studying or applying himself to the educational side of being a university student. To this day she admires his brilliant mind.

Ultimately as we know, he hitched his Motorbike behind his Austin Healey and drove to Salisbury. Once there, his pattern of six weeks of office work and six weeks' National Service, resumed. This time, however, he persuaded an elevated personage to allow him to assemble a Motor Cycle troop. He and his troop were on pedestrian border patrol and he believed and thus suggested; that he could design an effective silencer, to enable them to patrol much further and more effectively every day, on Motorbikes than on foot. So, he experimented with a bike silencer, achieving his goal. Thus, the Rhodesian Amy Motorcycle Troop was born.

For the next few years, he continued with his pattern of Military service and Civil Service in six-week cycles. He got to know his country's borders intimately and earned a great reputation at work. His Austin Healey became active in the Clubman motor racing Class at Donnybrook Track. He rode his motorbike at Scramblers. Motor racing has always been his passion. To this day, he avidly watches all the Formula One meets on Television.

## Chapter Thirteen
## Zionism

*Genesis 22:15-18 "Then the Angel of the Lord called to Abraham a second time and said; 'By Myself, I have sworn says the Lord, because you have done this thing and have not withheld your son, your only son – Blessings I will bless you, and multiplying I will multiply your descendants, as the stars of the heaven and as the sand on the seashore…;'"*

During these years Solveig was stationed on a Kibbutz in the Jordan Valley just South of the Sea of Galilee, better known in the region as Yam Kinneret. She travelled to and from Jerusalem when she could, or to Tiberias, Tel Aviv, Caesarea, Nazareth and Haifa. She loved the life of walking in the land where so much Biblical history had taken place. She swam in the Yam Kinneret, the Jordan River and the Dead Sea and in a desert cave near Wadi Qel (sic) where the phosphorus sparkled emeralds in the water deep under the golden-coloured rock. She hiked through the steep wadi and saw the monastery built into the cliff face over the cave where the Prophet Elijah hid, and was fed by ravens as recounted in the Bible. She once travelled with a group up north to Mount Hermon on the border with Syria and Lebanon. From there flows the Jordan River. In a pool at the bottom of a cliff cascade, there are myriads of tiny flesh-nibbling fishes. You can sit on the grass, and dangle your feet in the water. At first, it feels weird when the little fishes are gently sucking at your skin, but what a refreshing restorative pedicure it is!

Her working life on the Kibbutz varied. It was a large Kibbutz on the border with Jordan, with industry as well as a large quantity of varied agricultural productivity. Thus, she picked grapes, worked in the factory producing anodised stainless steel, and ironed piles of shirts in the laundry while hearing first-hand stories of life in concentration camps during WW2. She peeled potatoes from the twenty Kilo bag as well as the same amount, of onions. She has never forgotten how she cried over those onions. On several occasions she cooked eggs for the residents on a Saturday evening. The Kibbutz population numbered about three hundred people. Each person received two fried eggs, or scramble or omelette as requested. It was hectic and fun!

She experienced mechanised milking that was so very efficient. The high-tech, dairy still impresses her in memory, although she knows now that it is commonplace these days. It was not then, in her experience at any rate.

The farm also grew grapefruits, dates, table grapes, and cotton, and later also planted avocado pears and paw-paws known as papayas. Having a large dairy herd, there was also plenty of land planted for fodder crops. In these she spent some time manhandling massive irrigation pipes into position.

Nowadays she realises with more gravity the situation she was living in. She took for granted that all the people carried Uzi weaponry wherever they went. She was taken to a firing range and taught to handle a weapon herself. She took for granted that there were underground shelters and a constant threat of cross-border raids from Jordan and Syria. Now as a retired woman writing all this down, she is shaking her head in amazement. Oh, the ignorance of youth!

There was so much more. Desperate to read, she read the story of the Entebbe hi-jacking and rescue in French, before she was proficient in Hebrew. The kibbutz library had nothing in English. This achievement of reading a whole book in French so long after leaving school thrilled her and encouraged her to do more of the same. This was not too long after her next-door neighbour in the residence, had been the commanding officer in that remarkable and still fabled, rescue operation. The book had been published and distributed very fast.

She visited Jericho and walked round and around the ruins thinking of the ancient tribes marching around the walls of the fabled town for seven days before, on the final day, a trumpet blast caused the walls to crumble. Later she visited an archaeological dig in Jericho and had a look at the layers of exquisite mosaic floors that were having dust brushed off them. With a tour group, she climbed the ancient Masada ruins where the siege by the Romans of the last Jewish stronghold took place. Another archaeological dig, Tel Makor was visited twice. The first time she saw it they had uncovered fourteen layers of civilisations. Two years later, she visited it again and they had dug through to twenty civilisations. At one time in Jerusalem, she spent a day in the museum and also visited the dome of the book where the Dead Sea Scrolls were to be seen.

She spent six months at practical Hebrew classes known as Ulpan, and came out of it with accolades, for writing an essay that was not only language correct but was also a story of her dream of how the discovery of oil, perhaps in the Negev, could enhance the economy in Israel. Little did she know that at that time there were already two oilfields in the Sinai which had to be surrendered to Egypt in exchange for peace after the Yom Kippur war which was still very fresh in the minds of the young soldiers that had fought in the long desert battles in the quest to take Egyptian territory. Bear in mind, that she was there a long time ago, in the mid-nineteen seventies.

Since she was showing all signs of becoming a permanent resident, she was given the daytime work of childminding and also had to take on night watch duties from time to time like everyone else.

Twice interrupting her two-year stay in Israel, fleeing the incredible heat of the summers in the lowest spot on the earth, she travelled to Europe to indulge her love of history and art and the beauty of all the old architecture. On one occasion in the company of Hebrew and French speakers, she had a difficult but successful evening translating the conversation between the two groups. The following day she started her aerogramme home to Mum with the startling discovery that she was struggling to summon the English language to mind, as she had not spoken it for a very long time, and was having trouble with the mental shift.

Then once back on the Kibbutz, an accumulation of incidents caused her to doubt whether she could live thuswise for the rest of her life. Temperatures in high summer with the humidity of the Jordan valley soared into the late forties and even one night into the fifties centigrade, which effect is to make one feel weightless and disoriented. Granted that Israel was a new and developing "experiment" struggling for survival and wracked with wars, she realised that she simply did not have the stamina to commit her whole life to the country after all. At one time she had contracted Cholera and thought she might actually die there far away from her family.

No matter how much she loved Israel and the people there, or how much she loved the cultures of the holocaust survivors and their younger generations, she occasionally found it difficult to fit in socially. All attempts to understand Judaism and Zionism did not help her fit in with the culture and society. All her generation was comprised of war veterans whom she greatly admired, but found the people somewhat guarded and abrupt. This was also not to mention the extreme poverty of the general population of the townsfolk at the time. Although there was nothing special about her family's economic social status, she had been raised to expect a better standard of living and realised with horror and disgust that she was a bit of a snob. She was shocked by her attitude.

Somehow the fairy had disappeared from the tale. Comprehending that, because she had no love for South Africa's politics of the day, and did not want to "go home"; she felt lost and out of her comfort zone, with no idea where to go from there. She decided she would investigate whether she could get work in England. She responded to a Washington Post advertisement to train as a nurse at St Mary's in London and was surprised to be accepted.

From time to time during all of this, she and Alan had shared the odd communication. She wrote and told him of the plan to go and nurse in London. Within a very short time, he somehow got the phone number of the Kibbutz and called her. The gist of the call was "stop running away and come to Rhodesia". This she did with some alacrity.

## Chapter Fourteen
## Dubliners

*"Not enjoyment and not sorrow
is our destined end or way
But to act, that each tomorrow, Find us further than today."*

*Longfellow – A Psalm of Life*

Ireland in brief

British rule in Ireland began with the Anglo-Norman invasion of Ireland in 1069

Lordship of Ireland occurred between 1171 – 1542

Kingdom of Ireland (Under English rule) 1542 – 1800

United Kingdom of Great Britain and Ireland 1801 – 1922

Northern Ireland was merged with England under Great Britain 1801-1923

Irish resistance using guerrilla tactics was continuous.

Currently, the Republic of Ireland exists with a small section in the North still under British rule.

The Cordner land in Argentina had been claimed and developed by a couple from Dublin. These were Edward Ellis Cordner originally from Dublin, and Caroline Eugenie

Thacker also from Dublin. They had been briefly introduced to one another during the summer season in August 1873. Caroline was a stunningly beautiful woman from a family of means. The Cordner family originally hailed from Staffordshire as landed gentry but their ancestors were removed from the land after the Norman Conquest and given land in North East Ireland. As a minor son without hope of inheriting his father's estates Edward is listed as having been a comfortable businessman of some means, employed as a Financial Secretary in a large insurance and investment advisory company in Dublin. He had attended Grammar School in England attaining an excellent education and a mannerly bearing. Thereafter he studied Classics, Mathematics and History at Oxford before returning to Dublin.

The Thacker ancestors are recorded as having originated in Essex and it seems they were awarded land in Ireland for not resisting the Norman invasion. The Irish "troubles" were intensifying and coming to a crescendo and it was no longer comfortable or safe to be English and of means in Ireland on their country estate. They had retreated to Dublin where there was a semblance of law and order and a more gracious life in society. At that time Ireland was also reeling from successive potato blights and many of the poor were emigrating, either fleeing the hardships of constant Guerrilla warfare or the poisonous blight in the soil. Those with large country estates were finding them difficult to manage and their mansions began to deteriorate.

Caroline Eugenie Thacker's parents, Colonel Robert Thacker and Sarah Caroline Thacker (neé Bewley) were thus also residents in the county of Dublin. They had been married in the glorious church of the Holy Trinity in October 1851. Their daughter Caroline Eugenie's birth is registered in Harold's Cross Registry, Dublin on 3rd April 1855. They lived in Dún Laoghaire the smart Southern Suburb, in County Dublin. Around that time Dún Laoghaire became a small sailing craft harbour, and there was easy access to Black Rock beaches, famous for summer weekends away from home.

The Thacker family owned a seaside cottage at Black Rock, as did the Cordners. Both families enjoyed waterfront Summers, sailing and promenading on the harbour front taking the fresh sea air as it blew in across the Irish Sea from Welsh Holyhead. Generally, the waters were placid and warm being on the continental shelf and protected by the landmasses of Wales and Ireland in St George's Channel. During winter, however, lashing rain and gusting wind made the cliff walks more of an adventure for the hardy.

On one of these summer holidays to Black Rock, Caroline again met Edward Ellis Cordner. They recalled having met before, but dimly, and as they walked on the cliff promenade, viewing the sea and feeling the breezes on their faces and in their hair, they found common interests as they talked. Edward had thought she was lovely when he met her at several of the balls and had even danced with her, yet she had seemed distant. In truth, his reserved nature had not swept her off her feet. But during this summer at Blackpool, after intervening years during which both had matured, they found many shared interests in poetry, music and literature, after engaging in hours of conversation.

The two families entertained one another at their summer homes and went out for an occasional picnic tea together. Love blossomed and after a whirlwind romance, they married in the Anglican Cathedral of St Saviour in Dún Laoghaire on August 16$^{th}$ 1883. The bride was beautifully decked out in imported cream Chantilly lace and satin, carrying a generous bouquet of soft summer daisies and trailing greenery.  She was twenty-eight years old. Her parents were ever so happy to have gently nudged her off the proverbial shelf and were eager for the appearance of the first grandchild.

In the interim, having not found any suitor to her particular liking during the season of 1873 Caroline had trained as a teacher and spent some years working in a junior school for young ladies in Dún Laoghaire. This experience would later stand her in good stead.

Edward and Caroline settled in a comfortable semi in Dublin on Merrion Crescent. However; he had always dreamed of living on the land. Having been raised on a large estate with well-stocked stables, profuse gardens and manicured lawns, with hillsides for hunting and the Christmas shoot, this kind of life was what he yearned for. The Irish "troubles" were intensifying and coming to a crescendo and it seemed appropriate to plan a move to newer pastures. He knew that his preferred lifestyle could no longer be sustained in Ireland. They discussed relocation at length. He wanted to live on the land, but without an inheritance to rely on, he would need to amass a small fortune through his chosen profession which was not really likely. However, Caroline's father had provided her with a generous dowry, aware that Edward was not likely to inherit.

Together they plotted and planned and they had finally decided to move before they realised that she was expecting a child. Due time passed and their first child, a son named Percival was born in May 1884. He was a bonny bouncing boy and the pride and joy of his father who now had an heir. He was delighted with his beautiful wife's achievement. The birth of their son delayed the decision to relocate. They still had not decided where they would ultimately like to go. The Thacker parents were delighted with their grandson and Sunday lunches at the Thacker home after the late church service, became a regular occasion. This was to save Caroline the preparation of the repast, allowing her time to enjoy her child in the family setting.

There were thoughts and discussions of possibly relocating to Cape Town in South Africa, where the Huguenots had developed vineyards in a very conducive climate. At other times the romance of the new cities of Bulawayo and Salisbury in Rhodesia where Cecil John Rhodes had claimed the land for Queen Victoria, seemed attractive. Many mining opportunities were being developed in a land seemingly crowded with valuable minerals beneath the surface of rich red soil.
There is a range of hills named the Great Dyke where a notable collection of metal ores and valuable substances, lie underground for extraction.

Yet great Queen Victoria had declared that it was no longer a good idea to continue colonising the world at large. It was some time before the British actually created a form of government in Northern and Southern Rhodesia. They had heard of the beautiful Victoria Falls, a massive cascade into a deep curving gorge on the Zambezi River. Due to the project of building a railway bridge over the gorge to connect Northern and Southern Rhodesia, two small villages were developing, one aptly named after the Queen and the other being called Livingstone after Dr David Livingstone the intrepid explorer and missionary.

Edward continued to work in the city gaining a strong reputation for his dedication and expertise in financial matters and Caroline kept a fine home and enjoyed her baby son Percy. In the early months of 1886, Caroline was pregnant again. Now all she hoped for was a little girl for her pigeon pair. She started a girlish layette production, all the while tending to Percy as he became more agile running about, as his speech improved. He seemed to be an intelligent child and Edward enjoyed reading to him, even as he was climbing onto and over and under things tirelessly. He just could not sit still. As speech rapidly evolved, the questions never stopped.

In late November 1886, Caroline's second pregnancy came to term. She laboured long and with increasing trauma. The midwife attending bathed her forehead soothed her and sang to her to help her relax and not fight the pain. Then she prayed. Caroline writhed in agony and the infant refused to appear. Eventually, a doctor was called in who determined the problem and attempted to assist. But it was more than he thought. As Caroline yelled in pain the baby's head appeared, and as it emerged the source of the problem was found. The cord was caught around the infant's neck. Sadly, the process of emerging life was impeded by horrible strangulation and the baby was stillborn. They named her Eileen Sarah, posthumously.

A few days later there was a funeral out of Saint Saviour's where they had married. Oh, how they mourned! Caroline was heartbroken and also not well for some time. Her mother came to stay for a while to take care of Percy and to nurse Caroline back to strength. Then there was milk fever but "nana" knew the heated cabbage leaf remedy, and soon all pressure subsided. Then depression set in. Poor Caroline! She struggled with sorrow and exhaustion made worse by sleeplessness. All the while she berated herself for being less than a woman for failing at childbirth and less than a mother for needing help with her son.

The following summer they went to Blackrock. The Thacker family and the Cordners spent time relaxing together enjoying the mild temperatures and soft sea breezes. Walking the clifftops and enjoying the sea views can only be described as medicine for the soul. Little Percy was in his element. Edward helped him down the path onto the beach where they collected shells and paddled in the sea. Then Caroline joined them one morning and the morning sunlight seeped into her spirit and she started healing.

That evening she sat with her Bible reading the book of Proverbs, preparing herself for the task of raising a God-fearing son. This became a daily habit. She wanted to memorise every bit of wisdom she could. During late September, they all returned to Dún Laoghaire for the winter season.

That Christmas they decorated a tree and filled a stocking at the end of Percy's bed. After the morning service, the Cordner and Thacker families all celebrated Christmas Dinner at the Thacker Residence. It was a very jolly event. On Boxing Day, a parlour piano was delivered to the Cordner house for Caroline. The delight shone out of her like sunshine breaking through dark thunderclouds. A new season of joy began for Caroline. She had always played but on leaving home the family piano had remained in the family residence.

Edward had realised that her music would uplift her and also by osmosis fill them all with joy. Edward also played, so there was much music in the home. Percy was a bright child and he learned everything his parents taught him, greedily absorbing information. At the age of five, he was at the piano tinkering at nursery rhymes and playing snatches of church hymns from memory.

At age six he went off to the local school Glengara Park, where Miss Darling who had been a first-year student and friend of Caroline's while the latter was already an assistant headmistress, at her school for young ladies, was now a new staff teacher. Percy walked to school with Edward for the mornings and was fetched by Caroline at midday at the end of lessons. Thuswise Caroline and Miss Darling were acquainted.

Soon he was reading his bedtime storybooks to himself. During the summer of the same year, the Cordners went to Black Rock for the holidays. Edward took Percy out on a small sailboat on a day when the sea was clear and still and the wind very gentle. This minor early-age introduction to sailing lodged itself in Percy's soul and it became a lifelong delight.

## Chapter Fifteen
## Edward in Business

*"Be strong! Be good! Be Pure! The right only shall endure;
All things else are but false pretences."*

*Longfellow – The Golden Legend*

During that winter Edward was invited to take on a directorship in the company he was working with. This increased his monthly income as well as his pensionable options. He was delighted.

Percy began formal piano lessons with a teacher at his school. Edward bought a mare pony for him and liveried her at a small farm on the outskirts of town where the suburbs were greener. She was called "Pound" and was round of belly, dark and shiny of coat, with a good long mane, and a tail that swept the ground behind her. On Saturdays, Edward gave him lessons in a dressage ring.

Occasionally Edward and Caroline returned to their musings about seeking their fortune in a foreign land. They briefly considered America which was indeed an option and seemed to be where everyone was headed. They were even tempted by news of the Gold Rush. But the thought of traversing all those miles across a fairly undeveloped continent gave them considerable pause. There were also wild stories of gunfighting which simply did not appeal to these gently bred citizens. And then, putting a pause to the dreams of travel, was the realisation that another baby was on the way.

During this pregnancy, Caroline wisely rested and chose her meals carefully. She avoided wine and took only gentle exercise, walking in the cool of the evening. And she prayed earnestly for the health and strength of the baby. Losing a child had increased her awareness of her dependency on God the Father. Just before Christmas of 1886, Caroline delivered baby Lilian Eugenie. She was a thin baby, always energetically kicking and wriggling, with her arms waving and baby fingers pointing, her face archly engaging of expression. She was an early developer and greedy at the breast, often suffering from evening colic as a result. She was up and crawling at seven months and stood before her first birthday, walking a few days later.

Percy loved her to distraction, spending a lot of time down at her level on the floor engaging in simple play with her. He sat her on his lap when he played his piano pieces at practice and she squealed with delight. Edward and Caroline watched this fondly. It wasn't long before Lilian's little hands were also thumping piano ivories changing the key of the scales between Percy's practising hands.

Caroline then sat with Lilian and at that very young age taught her simple five-finger exercises and basic sol-fah. They sang scales arpeggios and sol-fah exercises together and this delighted Lilian who once she had learned the patterns sang them all day and often at night when in her crib before she slept. Fondly Edward and Caroline imagined their daughter singing parlour songs, or perhaps even training for opera. They were so grateful for their talented children.

Now that the mourning was over for Eileen, and Percy and Lilian were doing so well, Edward again turned his mind to becoming a landlord somewhere. Ownership of land had become a fundamental need approaching obsession and a reason for living. He dreamed of his ideals at night and chewed on his pen as he paused in calculations at work. He identified with acreage and fine living and longed for the respect that would be associated with land ownership. The more he dreamed, the more restless he became and the more he hated his desk job.

He began to hate the beautiful city of Dublin and even Dún Laoghaire lost its lustre. As his family grew, he began to resent the crowdedness of his home and to crave wide open spaces and the freedom of hunting and clay pigeon shooting and riding to hounds. To ease his longing, he took to walking long distances along the harbour and the river Liffey of an evening, returning home late for his evening tea.

His frustration and self-pity grew. At night he slept badly, dreaming fitfully of being boxed in and imprisoned. In the mornings he woke tired and grumpy. Caroline was dismayed as she observed the changes in her husband. Then she was pregnant again and the knitting, sewing and needlepoint were resumed. Her mother Sarah Thacker visited often, charmed by the growing family of grandchildren. She brought gifts of little garments and "receiving-shawls", along with supplies of cotton napkins.

In 1891 Caroline delivered another daughter and they called her Winifred Caroline. The baby thrived and appeared to be as quick-witted and alert as Percy and Lilian had been. She too was much loved and petted by her brother but her older sister Lilian was jealous of her. She would sneak up to the crib when she thought she was unobserved and smack the baby causing wails of distress. These wails resulted in the little one being petted by her mother and brought to the breast for comfort suckling. It has been said that the third child in a family suffers a certain sense of otherness and that they combat this insecurity by becoming forthright, bossy and ambitious.

Each of the children occupied their unique space in the family according to their personalities.

Sibling rivalry is a normal characteristic in family structures and develops uniquely in each family individually, affecting the development of the personalities in the group. Lilian was clearly a "special" child because of her obvious talents and delicate prettiness. Winifred felt very second best and sought ways to shine. As she learned to talk, she excelled in commandeering attention with words. She stored every word and its meaning in her head as soon as she heard it and became quite loquacious. She was sounder of stature than Lilian and somehow, in spite of the age difference she commandeered Percy into her "team".

Lilian slowly descended to third place in the sibling rivalry stakes. Her talent and delicacy made her gentle and unassertive and she withdrew into her private world apart from that inhabited by Percy and Winifred.

## Chapter Sixteen
## Argentina

*"Trust no future, however pleasant! Let the dead past bury its dead! Act – act in the living present! Heart within, and God o'erhead."*

*Longfellow – A Psalm of life*

Then one day it happened! It was during early 1892 that Edward saw a column in the newspaper detailing the amazing developments taking place in Argentina. And he mentioned it to his fellow financiers in the office. They two were aware of this and the Managing Director called a meeting in which he laid out his idea of opening up an office in Buenos Aires. There were also concerns about the politico-economic shifts occurring in Europe with all the unification processes and constant shifting of alliances. People began to worry about possible wars. Many considered it a good business move to operate in Argentina. The Managing Director looked around the room making eye contact with each person at all levels of seniority. Was there anyone in the room willing to pack up and relocate? Edward was.

He had reached the end of his tether and simply needed to leave his "terrace house" on a "suburban street" and exchange it for wide open spaces and the possibility of land ownership. Deep down in his very soul and self-perception, he knew he was entitled to be a landlord which the fact of his birth order had denied him what he deemed his place in life to be. As a second son in the British aristocracy, if that is what he indeed was, it is a difficult position to be in.

It breeds jealousy and competition between brothers. This can either build or break a man. In his opinion, his brother did not have what it took to be a lord of the manor house on a gracious estate. He could not inherit his family home with all its history, but he could acquire land and build a new tradition for Percy to inherit!

Edward was more than ready to travel to Buenos Aires and do whatever was required of him to match his dreams in the new world. He had complete belief in his ability to successfully open a new office, and grow a healthy clientele.

It was suggested then that Edward should pack up and travel immediately to Buenos Aires and open up an office and then send for his family. He demurred on the grounds that he had three children and it was unfair to expect his wife to pack up their home and travel alone. After much discussion Edward and his secretary would go on ahead to establish an office, and employ some staff and then when Edward felt secure, he would return to fetch his family and bring them out. And that is how it happened.

Before his departure, Edward visited his father and spoke of his dreams and ambitions as well as his desire to make the family name good in Argentina. He expressed the wish to establish an estate in the accepted landed English style as well as a church and parsonage. This appealed to his father whose dreams of furthering the family "empire" inspired him to promise to wire funds to Edward, for the purpose of establishing an estate as envisaged, once he had a bank account in Buenos Aires.

With all due haste a berth on a ship was booked and with only several valises of clothing and a briefcase each, he and Patrick his secretary, were off! It had been established that there were many ships plying the seas between Europe, Britain and Argentina due to the massive economic growth and development occurring there.

Edward was as good as his word. He and his secretary, Patrick had a good relationship and worked well together. Immigration was swift and efficient albeit in Spanish with the help of an interpreter. Permission to trade was granted and they found lodgings and searched diligently for appropriate office space to rent. The office in Ireland wired funds to cover expenses and within two weeks they opened for business.

Both attended Spanish language classes several evenings a week. Patrick was younger and unmarried so he also was out and about getting to know local women. This activity helped his language development dramatically. Slowly they developed some clientele, mostly from other foreign companies opening up in Buenos Aires.

In the interim Edward set about looking for a property that he could develop, that could fulfil his dreams of being landed gentry, in this new country. Near his rental home, he had identified undeveloped land. In his mind's eye there rose before him a charming Anglican church. He approached the council offices and asked about zoning and various regulations. The plot was level and well-placed in the suburb of Quilmes. His luck was in. It appeared that the council had set that land apart for a church and they were delighted to discuss his ideas.

Having made some rough sketches of what he hoped to build, he identified an architectural/engineering partnership and approached them for plans. Together they visited the site. This new relationship resulted in them becoming clients of the Insurance House/Financial Accounting/Investment Advisory Service office, he and Patrick were developing. Within a month, plans were drawn and submitted, and the Church Council in England had been approached about the authorisation and dedication of a church. They would also need a Vicar. Cordner Senior transferred the first deposit to Edward's account. For his father's investment purposes, Edward devised a method of costing the project within which to budget the development as it progressed. Building work on the church began and progressed well according to plan.

 The foundations were of hewn stone and the floor was of an exquisitely laid pattern of cut stone. Yet in the long run, it was not financially feasible to complete in stone, and the building was raised in brick and mortar, with the internal arches and vaulting details finished with graceful moulded plastering and paintwork. The foundation stone was laid in December 1891. It is not a large church but is beautifully designed in the interior though rather plain on the exterior. Perhaps gardens were planned but not completed. There is a simple clock tower entrance with a cross on top of the edifice, the usual nave and raised altar apse. The Eastern apse has arched embrasures for which Edward ordered stained glass window panes. The land was too small to include transepts. The church was ultimately dedicated and named "All Saints".

The great volume of shipping passing through, ensured that mail delivery was efficient, and Edward regaled Caroline on his daily activities and she responded in kind. All in all, Edward was away for two and a half years before he felt it was possible to return and bring his family to their new home. He booked passage on a vessel due to sail within a month and he occupied the time before sailing by searching for a home. He rented a large house in the area of La Plata, signed a year's lease, and paid rent for the year in advance; duly assisted by the company as promised by them. On the due date, he boarded the ship and began the journey home.

Having received an advance warning by mail, Caroline, assisted by her father and brothers packed up their belongings into crates. The piano was carefully wrapped and padded and crated with much waxing of the packing canvasses to protect it from moisture; dampness and salt. Their furniture and all carpets and linens, and metal and porcelain ware; were packed. Everything was labelled and delivered to the shipyard.

On the projected date Edward arrived and after visiting various family groups to bid farewell, Edward spent some time with his father describing the progress of the Church development. Edward had not heard from the church council in England so his father agreed to find a Vicar and ensure his arrival in Buenos Aires as soon as he could arrange it. Accordingly, he and Caroline with their three children and all their belongings finally set sail. They and all their goods took one ship from Dublin to Liverpool and from Liverpool to Southampton. In Southampton docks all their belongings were transferred to the hold of another ship named the Danube, eliciting vivid thoughts of Viennese waltzes.

On January 16$^{th}$ 1893, the Danube set sail towards Buenos Aires. They sailed Saloon class with glee as they embarked on the great adventure.

Yet still, there was sorrow. During the journey young Lilian, the shining talent of the family, but always delicate in stature, succumbed to pneumonia and sadly passed away in spite of efforts on the part of the ship's doctor to save her. She was buried at sea in a simple ceremony. The harsh part of a sea burial is, that the deceased disappears into the water never to be seen again. There is no grave to visit and mark with a stone, where flowers can be left on anniversary dates. These are inscribed on the heart and in the family Bible.

There had been so much sorrow. Caroline was not well and blamed it on grief and nervous exhaustion due to the general upheaval of removals and unaccustomed sea travel. Then she realised that she was actually pregnant. However, she did not have time to focus on pregnancy as she was still mourning the loss of little Lilian. Edward was very subdued too. One never recovers from the death of a child, and Percy and Winifred were also gravely affected by the loss of Lilian. Percy in particular berated himself for not spending more time with her since the arrival of his younger sister. Winifred was too young to understand the pang of emptiness her sister had left. Her response to her pain and confusion was temper tantrums.

When they arrived in Buenos Aires, the city was blooming lilac with masses of flowering Jacarandas. Caroline was captivated by the colour and the way they carpeted the ground below as the blossoms fell. Just as soon as they arrived, Edward shepherded his family through formal immigration procedures into Argentina and claimed their belongings from the docks; arranging for the delivery to the house he had rented.

Happily, everything arrived without damage. Edward proudly arranged transport and escorted his family to their new rental home. He hired professional movers to open the crates and unpack their belongings and bring all furnishings and soft goods into the rented house overlooking the sea. On the first night, it was a little chaotic and strange but exhaustion and the emptiness of Lilian's absence resulted in sleep although of restless quality. Within the first week, a piano tuner was called to attend to the instrument which was the heart of the family. Edward hoped that the resumption of music in the home would brighten the family's mood.

The commissioned stained-glass windows for the church arrived and were carefully fitted. Everyone agreed that they were most beautiful, in particular with the morning light streaming through the ones in the Eastern apse. Then he received notification from Ireland that the ordained Son of the local Vicar was on his way to take up the living in the Vicarage. Edward purchased a small house near the church. He regretted that it had not been possible to actually build it on the same property as the church.

Caroline's pregnancy advanced. This time around she took it all in her stride. In spite of the trauma of the early months, she carried well. She bloomed and was energetic and beautiful even as she took upon herself the appearance of a ship in full sail. She was busy and confident and looking forward to another child.

Though she had married late and was older than most when her first child was born, she prided herself in her success as a wife and mother. All too soon the day of delivery came and she birthed successfully at home in the rented house in La Plata, assisted by a local midwife. All went well. Baby Emma Violet arrived in late August of 1893.

During the same week, the roof of the church was finally sealed and waterproofed. Carpenters had been building the pews and the pulpit as well as an Altar and Baptismal Font, which were all polished conscientiously, with beeswax and turpentine by assistants. In a rush, the dedication of the Anglican Church of All Saints took place, even as the Altar carvings were still not fully polished. The first service after the official Dedication was Emma's Baptism, which is registered as occurring on October 1st 1893.

## Chapter Seventeen
## La Elvira, "La Matanza"

*"Strange is the heart of man
with its quick mysterious instincts!"*

*Longfellow – The Courtship of Miles Standish*

Now that he had achieved his first goal of the development of a church and Vicarage, and had found a Vicar dependent on him for a living, Edward's next step was to scout for his Estate. He was able to purchase on a plan that deferred title until annual payments finally covered the stated price. The government reserved the right to award or defer title if the land was worked well and showed a profit, or to reclaim it if it did not bear the fruits of the enterprise.

This property comprising some eighty hectares, lies inland from Quilmes, near enough to the coast to be fed by moisture from the sea. The climate is mild but the Land and sea breezes blow, influenced by the changing temperatures between land and sea, during day and night, often causing certain tree types to bend permanently as a result of prevailing sea winds.

The Cordners were to find the summers warm and winters cool. It was lovely land in the area that was called "La Matanza", in which was an abandoned farm, called "La

Elvira." The grass was rich, evidencing good soil, and beyond the lower hill country, rose the distant majestic mountain ranges in the far-off west, that on clear days, were a joy to behold. Sunsets were glorious above the distant mountains in the evening and on clear mornings, the shapes of towering rock could be seen, glowing rose, then gold, as the sun rose in the East. Edward knew in his heart that this was his calling, and his lifelong dream had been realised. Yet he dared not stop working in the city until he was established on the land; so he threw himself into the challenge with a will that would have astonished his father.

As we know, Edward's office in Buenos Aires acquired custom from a large Civil Engineering company, working in cooperation with a firm of Architects. They had recently become involved with the development of roads, bridges and the new railway line, hugging the picturesque coast beside a planned auto-touring route along the Bahia Blanca. This was further South of the city, on a coastal promontory headland, where the scenic coastline lent itself to the development of tourism-related hotels and mansions for the wealthy as well as entertainment venues. He and Patrick and by now their several employees had become involved in this venture. It was some distance South of Buenos Aires city so Edward and Patrick rented a small cottage where either of them could sleep over if necessary to reduce travel. This was also shared with the site engineers.

He was really happy following his chosen accounting abilities but even more so, he was delighted to be indirectly involved with the picturesque developments of their customers. His natural mathematic abilities enabled him to measure building plans. Estimate costing and then during the project assist by advising where cost controls could be made. This ability that he demonstrated attracted developers to seek him out, and was a boon to the company he was working with. This was, unbeknownst to him, the forerunner of modern-day Quantity Surveying.

His land was near enough to the growing town of Buenos Aires to ultimately allow Edward to work in the city and live in a rural setting. He acquired a sturdy, Argentinian-built, limited-edition motor vehicle, called "Anasagasti Tourer", as he needed to be able to travel some distance in a given day in the line of his different activities.

The family continued living in the Quilmes district to the South of Buenos Aires, in La Plata, while Edward started his long-term project of developing the estate. There was a homestead, but it had become derelict and needed much work. Percy was old enough to enter an excellent Grammar school-type boy's boarding college, so Edward enrolled him at Saint Basile – Religieuses Hospitaliers at the beginning of the following school term.

The school was an establishment designed to develop gentlemen able to comport themselves in high society. Percy was ten years old. He had been well taught in Dublin at the Grammar school there, but suddenly having to study in Spanish medium was a shock to his young system. He had been provided by his parents with a comprehensive phrase book and an English/Spanish Dictionary. In all fairness, Edward had started speaking some Spanish to the children occasionally. Ahead of delivering Percy to the school, his parents spent time explaining what to expect, and encouraged him. They assured him that they believed, in his innate talent and intelligence, and that he would do well. They pointed out that having a musical ear usually helps people conquer new languages with apparent ease.

The education of the girls was left to Caroline since she was a teacher. She decided to arrange to attend Spanish classes for herself as soon as she was able to. Meanwhile, Edward was planning the first stages of redeveloping the original basic cottage on their "estate". He sketched a design similar to that of his family home on the estate in Ireland. It would be a double-storied home with two wings on either side of the great entrance hall and central staircase. Below the staircase, there would be a pantry and a kitchen with windows and doors to the rear of the house.

Mindful of the climate's warm summers, he designed a deep verandah to cool the kitchen and pantry and also allow a breezy spot where there would be a table and chairs from which views of the kitchen garden could be enjoyed. To one side of this would be a wood store and a laundry yard. On the other side, there would be accommodations for herdsmen known as cowboys, a few stables and space for a cart and land-work implements.

On one side of the hall in the front of the house, there would be the dining room and beyond that a conservatory. On the other side, there would be a Library, Music room and a sitting room with French doors opening onto a wide raised verandah that could shade the rooms in the heat of summer. Upstairs there would be four bedrooms and a study. Behind the ground floor living rooms, there would be bathroom and toilet facilities. Edward had identified a source of a faithful Argentinian copy of a "Thomas Crapper Water Closet" which had revolutionised home lavatorial health facilities. He planned to plumb a freshwater and wastewater system into bathrooms and kitchens. Once the house was complete, they would build stables and acquire some horses.

Edward could not wait to finish his project and invite his parents for a visit. Caroline had agreed to contribute to the costs with her dowry. They even dreamed of an arched portico and heavily carved wooden double doors at the entrance.

Realising that this was to be an expensive exercise, Edward approached a bank for a building loan. On the strength of his position at work, and the fact that he was contributing to a private pension plan, together with the deposit that would be paid using Caroline's dowry; the loan was approved. Within days he hired a building firm and ordered supplies from the building merchants. Sadly, he could not commit to building in stone and settled for brick and mortar, plastered and painted over.

The foundations were laid and built on beautifully cut stone blocks that would show above ground between the level of the yard, and the porches, designed to create a touch of shade from the sun to the front of the house. The term "verandah" was borrowed from India, and it is usually found between the home and garden areas of the house. There would be carved wooden architraves on doors and windows to add interest to the design indoors and out.

An expert would do the front portico and curved balustrades and finials on the stone front doorsteps. Soon building began. In his spare time, Edward laid out paddocks and personally built the wooden fences and whitewashed them. The lease for the house In La Plata was extended. The company covered the rent because of Edward's directorship and out of respect for the position he was carving for himself in society in Buenos Aires.

As the Cordner mansion slowly rose out of the ground, Edward saw to it that the stable block was built and hayfields were planted. At the agricultural fair, he bought four Clydesdales, three fillies and a stallion He first ascertained that their bloodstock was well varied, and they were all of a registered bloodline. A few months later, he bought the first of his planned sheep flock. At weekends the family visited the "estate" to view the developments at the house. Caroline began to fear that she would need some staff and began to worry about the costs. During school breaks, Percy was at home and he spent a lot of time with Edward, involved in the project.

A home farm would be required, so a landsman was employed, and a team of mules was acquired to work with the Clydesdales. Land work implements were bought and were temporarily stored in the stables, pending the building of the coach house, for that and other related draft equipment, that would be added to the stables, where the mules and carthorses were comfortably housed.

The farmer's brief was to ensure there was animal feed and a good plot of vegetables for the house. Edward also wanted a small dairy herd. The dream of Caroline's life had always been to have ducks for her egg production. The farmer, Pedro Quirinos was asked to arrange an earth dam to be built and stocked with a variety of breeding fish. A shelter was built for the duck nesting places.

This different life was very exciting and Edward relished the way he was taming their immediate environment and developing their elegant house and home farm. Then, as the small conifers and tender young oak and apple trees Edward had been encouraging to grow, were flourishing and growing taller, Caroline found she was pregnant again. But at only a couple of months in, she miscarried and realised that perhaps she was now past childbearing age. She had been feeling very tired of late.

At the house in La Plata, she spent her time teaching the girls to read, sew, and knit simple garments. She set them arithmetic tasks and taught them at the piano. The house was filled with music as there was always some family member trifling at the keys. Caroline devised duets for them so that they could play together. And when Percy was home for school holidays, he filled the house with the Beethoven Sonatas and Mendelssohn melodies, Songs Without Words that he had been learning during term time. He had grown so much and Caroline was very proud of her young son, now tall and handsome with the most beautiful manners, and speaking properly accented fluent Spanish.

The day finally arrived when they were able to transport all their furniture to the new house on the farm. But the large house echoed around them as they did not have curtain fabric lengths for the tall windows and sufficient carpeting nor even enough furniture. What had been adequate in La Plata left the large rooms echoing and cold. Edward brought catalogues home for them to look at. With the death of Queen Victoria, fashionable furnishing had changed in style.

This was to their advantage as furniture sales houses were filled with the large Victorian second-hand pieces selling at affordable prices, having been retired in favour of the new styles. Edward, Caroline and Percy with them, chose furnishings from catalogues and placed their orders. Of course, the furniture then had to be paid for and packed and crated and delivered by sea. It took a couple of months, but eventually, they were able to go to the shipyard warehouses and arrange for the delivery of their purchases.

Their Argentinian friends were baffled by the way they clung to the old styles. There was plenty of beautiful furniture in the classic Spanish style available, made locally by Spanish master craftsmen in Buenos Aires. Caroline was perfectly happy to use Spanish brocades and velvets for soft furnishing and drapes. The colours were rich and vibrant and the silks from the east were also lovely for pretty detailed cushion covers and day table covers. With the move finally effected Edward wanted to host a dinner party to introduce his business contacts to one another in his lovely new home.

For this event they each had new clothes made. Percy was kitted out in a tailored suit like his dad's and Caroline and the girls had similarly styled dresses made, though of course Caroline's was a full dinner gown. Winifred and Emma had frocks that were not floor length but were ever so pretty, with dainty dancing pumps on their feet. Caroline tied their hair in strips of cotton the night before to create lovely ringlets. A business associate had helped Edward to hire some excellent kitchen staff and a butler for the night, so that poor Caroline was not responsible for anything more than giving orders and setting the table. On the evening of the party, Percy played for the guests who were favourably impressed. A few of them suggested that he should learn some Spanish classics. He agreed to attend to this idea when back at school. The meal served received praise, and the guests were very jolly at the end of the evening when they all set off for home.

In the morning Edward wrote to his parents telling them of their first formal entertainment at their completed home and what a success it had been. He would love them to come and visit. He and Caroline felt the house seemed unfinished due to the dearth of paintings on the walls and sadly they had used candelabrum for lighting. He realised that it was high time that he arranged gas lights. He consoled himself with the thought that his family home had developed over centuries and his home was new and as yet unlived in and not yet imbued with tradition. In fact, in his eyes, it was an upstart poor imitation of what he had dreamed of. He consoled himself believing that the future ahead would hold many forthcoming generations.

## Chapter Eighteen
## Cordner Estancia

*"Happy thrice happy, everyone Who sees his labour well begun, and not perplexed and multiplied."*

*Longfellow – The Building of the ship*

The little family's early years on the Estate involved hard work. The home farm constantly needed fencing repairs and the first cattle and horses were bought for breeding and herded to the ranch by men on horseback from the sales in Buenos Aires. Caroline nurtured a vegetable patch laid out and planted by Pedro, as well as a rose garden, and struggled to encourage a Wisteria to cling to the porches of the back verandah, without success. Percy grew apace and seemed to always need longer trousers, and to have his shirt sleeves lengthened.

Edward introduced a puppy into the home for Percy to love and care for. There is nothing more joyful than a relationship between a boy and his dog in an environment where there is fresh air and light and space to run and play. Then Edward allocated one of the saddle horses to Percy to ride. Percy was pleased and when at home he rode out every day, with his dog following him and his mount. As his confidence increased, he rode further afield beyond their farm and became familiar with the surrounding countryside and their neighbours.

Her teaching years in Ireland had helped Caroline to get the girls through primary-level reading, writing and arithmetic. She taught them all manner of needlework, art and music. She involved them in the garden and taught them flower arranging and they sat together painting artfully laid out items of "objets d'art". She also taught them deportment and dance steps. There were regular hours spent in the kitchen learning to cook and bake, preserve and bottle.

Caroline loved to encourage the girls out into the sunshine and taught them to study nature, observing the flowers and the trees and the nesting birds and buzzing insects. A spider web in the morning dew through which the sun's rays shone, was a diamond spectacle that gave them much joy. Then one evening, Edward came home with a box in which nestled a couple of kittens. This gift of little furry friends was a source of great delight. One was a grey and black stripey ball of fluff with a pink nose and green eyes, and the other was a tortoiseshell whose eyes were already changing from green to gold. Emma chose the tortoiseshell to be her own and Winifred, immediately loved the striped kitten. Emma named her kitten Patches and Winifred's little treasure became Tiger Kitty. Of course, once the cats were house-trained all was well, but at first, it was a case of "look out for puddles and other deposits!"

At night the kittens snuggled in the girls' beds and the parents watched fondly from just out of sight as peace settled in the room. Moonlight would peep through the shutters and make light stripes on the opposite wall, and then the ceiling as the night wore on. During the evenings before bed, there were stories, fond memories of home, related by either parent, whichever took their turn. Caroline relived with them events of her youthful friendships and pranks in childhood, and also spoke of her family life with her parents in a land far away in the North. They listened attentively to stories of holidays at Black Rock and the seaside, and visits to George's Quay. She told them of the journey from Ireland via Liverpool and Southampton across the Atlantic to Buenos Aires and the work that went into their lovely home here on the farm here in Argentina. Edward made their eyes sparkle as he described his boyhood on the Irish estate and his first pony and then later his beautiful mare named Sooty. They told of the grandparents, of Edward's Father's lovely house and Estate.

When Percy was home Edward talked of his college years and his work in the city and Caroline told of her teacher training and years as a teacher. Percy decided that he would like to study in Dublin and from there onwards at Oxford.

Winifred admired her mother's teaching prowess and dreamed of becoming a teacher. It was decided to ultimately send the girls to a finishing establishment for young ladies in Buenos Aires, recommended by Donna Delgado; where they would have plenty of opportunities to hone their Spanish language skills. To reward him for his accomplishments at school, Edward took Percy to the sales to choose for himself a tall riding horse all his own.

Meanwhile, Percy who was considerably older than the girls remained aloof from all the feminine activities. Occasionally he went up to town with his father for a day but usually, went riding or spent time at the piano. Edward taught him marksmanship with a view to hunting trips sometime in the future. Emma and Winifred picked flowers, pressed them and glued them onto cards on which they inscribed Longfellow quotations and then set them in oval frames as had become the fashion.

As time passed, the beef herd grew in number, and thus increased grazing pasture was required, Edward leased more land and extended his operation. It was a quiet life as their neighbours were far-flung and often the only other people they interacted with, were farm assistants and herdsmen who rode out on horseback, controlling the wanderings of the cattle sheep and other horses. These were a mixed crew of Spanish Gauchos and Argentinian

"Mapuche" Indians, who lived in their own settlement, keeping to themselves socially, though the farmer had his own cottage where he lived with his young family.

Winifred was captivated by the horsemen galloping around ensuring that the cattle and sheep were where they should be. She thought the "cowboys" were very dashing in their leather chaps, boots with spurs and felt hats. The girls grew into young women and learned to keep the house, cooking and baking and mending, and creating lovely new garments for themselves. They also loved to observe the mounted men outdoors, often peering shyly from a hidden spot. In future years they were to entertain their children and grandchildren in Rhodesia with tales of life "on the Ranch" with the cowboys dashing around, creating a sense of adventuristic romance and panache.

Occasionally they all travelled to Buenos Aires to shop for shoes, fabrics and various delicate items, that could not be equalled by home crafting. These trips always included either a visit to the theatre, the opera, or a dance performance as well as a Sunday service in the church at Quilmes. For overnight accommodation, they tended to return always to the same boarding house run by the very kindly Spanish lady, who had become a friend, known as Donna Delgado, who happened also to be an artist. Her canvasses were vivid, bold depictions of the countryside, describing high mountain peaks in glorious sunsets, with the odd Spanish-style home featured in a quaint yard. She excelled at painting country scenes with magnificent clouds and watery reflections. Her talent was enviable and famed in Buenos Aires. On the odd visit, they acquired a painting from her and these hung in their home. Gradually Caroline chose and purchased a collection of paintings for the house. Then she commissioned portraits of each of them for posterity.

As a result, Donna Delgado visited the homestead on the estate where each family member in turn sat for their portrait. The artist's style was rich and vivid and she did justice to each portrait. Each was duly set in intricately carved wooden frames painted over with gilt. The result was simply magnificent. Later she returned and painted some horses and a view of the house and garden. These were hung in the downstairs rooms. At the age of sixteen Winifred travelled to Buenos Aires daily with Edward to attend teacher training college, excelling in spite of the fact that all but one course was taught in Spanish. The other was English literature and language style. After graduating she started teaching at a local school for young ladies in Quilmes.

Meanwhile, back at the ranch as they say, from time to time, gaucho couples would hold a dance-off to the exotic beats and strains of tango tunes near the farmer's homestead. Edward and his family would attend their flamboyant, colourful festivals. These were very happy years of assimilation into their surrounding culture.

At the time of writing; it occurs to the narrator that Caroline lived a sad life. Uprooted from her family and moved all the way to Buenos Aires, requiring her to apply herself to Spanish in South America. Accustomed to a refined society life in Dublin, she had become a nomad following her husband's dreams and ambitions. Her poor health resulting in the loss of several babies, and her life of relative isolation in the large house on La Elvira, bred in her feelings of quiet, unexpressed desperation. Her upbringing decreed that she always present a cheerful and decorous manner which masked a gradually deeper and more desperate sense of despair. Bred to be a society hostess, who somehow missed her calling due to having been uprooted and far removed, she always felt somewhat out of place and unfulfilled.

It seems that the Cordner family, headed by the aristocratic, socially and upwardly mobile, Edward; commandeered respect from their neighbours simply for the good community-minded people that they were. Their "Estancia" was successful and they were financially secure.

Sadly, Caroline passed away in 1913 leaving behind her son Percy aged twenty-seven and at the time back in Ireland. Winifred aged twenty-two years and Emma even younger, aged just twenty, also in Ireland at the time, were devastated by the loss of their loving, gentle mother and role model. Her death certificate cites severe anaemia and other related troubles. She was laid to rest in the churchyard at Quilmes "All Saints" that Edward had facilitated and a beautiful headstone records her memory as well as a lovely stained-glass window. There is also a memorial to the contribution the Cordners had made in the area.

There is no doubt that Edward adored his lovely wife, but it seems possible that the fact may not have been adequately communicated to her. He was not a man who returned from town of an evening, with fragrant roses and sparkling trinkets buried in silken negligees, tied up in glossy boxes and satin ribbons. He was too busy leaving his mark in the business world.

## Chapter Nineteen
## Eduardo and Winifreda

*"Sorrow and silence are strong and patient
Endurance is God-like."*

*Longfellow - Evangeline*

If you study a map of Argentina, you will notice that just North of the city of Santa Rosa situated to the west at a point about midway between La Plata and Bahia Blanca to the East, there are two points of interest. One is the village or outpost or station of Eduardo and nearby, to the South is a similar point called Winlfreda. The narrator finds this to be of great interest. It may be a completely unconnected coincidence, but it is interesting nevertheless. Somewhere in that district nestled the furthest Western reaches of the area known as La Matanza. Most of Edward's erstwhile land is now overrun by the suburban spread from the centre of the city of Buenos Aires, so today there is no sign of the farm. The manor house is possibly privately owned, and not recognisable in the suburbs.

The Boer wars in South Africa ending in late 1910 resulted in new arrivals of people not wishing to live under British Dominion. By 1912 their community had grown. Winifred was content with teaching where she only met parents and pupils, but Emma had met a young man who had been in Argentina doing business. Her eyes were starry with young love. Percy, now grown, was in Dublin finishing College, and soon to go off to Oxford.

Sydney Austen Cowper a young Architect, had come from Ireland to invest in the exciting economy of Buenos Aires and had met the enchanting young Emma during family trips to town and worshipping at All Saints Quilmes; and above all, through a business relationship formed with Edward Cordner through the Architectural/Engineering Partnership for whom he managed the financial investment accounts. Emma was sweet sixteen and had just started training as a teacher as had Winifred sometime before, but she knew Sydney was the man for her. Yet she was considered far too young for marriage by Edward.

The year was 1909. They spent time outdoors, going on outrides, in the countryside, and when he was over in the evenings for dinners they sat on the porch and dreamed the sort of dreams young lovers do. They were determined to marry and could speak of nothing else but their dreams of a glorious future together. In 1912 they were allowed to become engaged to marry. In 1913 they travelled to Ireland to meet his family and then whilst there, as the war began to be everything spoken of by everyone; she went to stay with her Thacker grandparents in Dublin. He enlisted to join the war. He was serving in the Naval Officer Corps. During a lull in operations, he took shore leave and returned to Dublin to marry Emma in 1916. In 1918 Emma delivered twin girls and called them Winifred and Patricia. It is worth noting here that Sydney's time on the seas had inspired wanderlust.

Word came that Percy had seen fit to marry his cousin Ida Cordner! Considerable consternation resulted among the family members. Edward realised immediately that through this, (dare we say it?) - "incestuous union" everything he had worked for, could not now be inherited by his son, due to the disgrace, and the unlikelihood that any grandchildren could possibly result. Edward's repeated invitations to his parents to visit met with silence and they never came.

He took consolation in the fact that Emma and Sydney Cowper were secure and that Sydney was a gentleman of means.

Back in Buenos Aires, "Winifreda" as she had become known by then, was thus alone with her father Edward, now known as "Eduardo"; her mother gone, Emma off to Ireland and Percy pursuing other things. New arrivals from South Africa were passing through. Occasionally one or two worked briefly as cowherds or assistant farmers on the Cordner land under Pedro. Hardened by relocation, warfare and much loss, they were rough around the edges and focused on rebuilding their lives. For some of them, life had never been comfortable. As soon as they had earned a few months' wages they moved on. They were searching for something else.

Occasionally she was unsuccessfully courted by one of these "birds of passage". They were toughened by guerrilla warfare, having trekked North from the Cape in search of land to settle on, and developed that land only to have to defend it not once, but twice from the British, leaving many of them embittered and harsh in attitude. On the one hand, she was attracted to their strength of will and their sad stories of loss, and on the other, she couldn't relate to their rough foreignness and guttural accents.

War had broken out in Europe, and many young able-bodied men went off to enlist, searching for adventure and glory. Most never returned from the carnage and horror that ended in 1918. In a way, poor Winifred seemed to have "missed the boat". Edward and Winifred were the known master and mistress of the estate, both contributing to the farm and both working in town.

After the war was over Mr and Mrs Sydney Austen Cowper decided to follow the many veterans that had befriended Rhodesians that served Britain and her allies during the war, and travelled to what was called by them; "God's own Country". Here there were many opportunities as had also been in Argentina. Sydney Austen Cowper had been born in South Africa of Irish descent and Educated at the most celebrated school there; Bishops for Boys, situated in Rondebosch, Cape Town.

He had been on holiday with school friends to Rhodesia and loved the place. While his parents had returned to Ireland, he dreamed of one day coming to live in Salisbury. Either there, or in the beautiful city of Bulawayo where there was the excitement of great development occurring. The beautiful wide streets are a testament to its development in the days when a team of sixteen needed space to turn round and travel the other way.

All of this had been communicated to Edward Ellis Cordner. Ever restless and of an adventuresome nature, Edward began to dream of the wonderful place called Rhodesia with the massive river that cascaded into a deep gorge in the town of Victoria. There the mighty tumbling river spray rises high into the sky and the sun shines on it making a rainbow, and even the moon at night allows rainbow colours. The local people call it "Thundering Smoke".

## Chapter Twenty
## Arrival of Andrew Young McCormick

*"By the fireside there are youthful dreamers building castles fair, with stately stairways; Asking blindly of the Future what it cannot give them,"*

*Longfellow – The Golden Milestone*

Around that time Andrew Young McCormick and his friend Sandro were wandering around looking for accommodation and occupations in the area of Buenos Aires known as "La Matanza". Andrew, born in Scotland, and raised in Chile and his friend Sandro a native of Chile, arrived at the Cordner Estancia as the year changed from 1918 to 1919. The two men were employed as Cowboys to tend the horses, sheep and cattle.

Daily Eduardo and Winifreda as they were now known, travelled to Buenos Aires to work, and in the evenings they returned. Their housekeeper Marta with the help of Ana ensured the house was always clean and tidy, and clothing and linen were laundered. Her sister Maria acted as cook and baker, preparing and serving all meals. The farm was ably managed by Pedro Quirinos. It was to him that Andrew and Sandro applied for work and were answerable.

Employees on the farm consisted of the three women in the house, and Andrew and Sandro were at the beck and call of the Argentinian farmer Pedro. There were also gardeners and stable hands. Apart from Pedro who had his own home and cottage garden, that he shared with his family, the rest were fed from the homestead kitchen

Thus, Edwardo and his daughter Winifreda were alone. Andrew (sometimes known as Andreja) and Sandro, with names that seemed to match and almost rhyme; were now busily employed taking care of the animals and assisting on the farm. However, due to Andrew being more or less from the old country, he and his companion were made welcome on a friendly level over and above the status of "cowboys". Sandro and Andrew grew into the habit of loitering at the homestead in the evening on the wide back verandah chatting with Edward and Pedro the manager, sometimes joined by Winifred when she was not busy with other things. Occasionally the men heard her at the piano indoors.

Andrew was a little rough around the edges but had an interesting story and all the right capabilities. He blossomed under the attention of Win, quietly observed by Sandro who did not feel comfortable with the developing social rift between them.

Over time, Andrew adopted social graces and spoke in cultured tones when in the Cordner's company, with his accent still carrying the Scots brogue of his father Alexander's origins, blended with the curious lisping habit all Spanish speakers in South America developed. He charmed Winifred and Edward alike, with exotic tales of his boyhood adventures in the wild country of the forests, plains and mountains of Chile. He spoke vividly seemingly oblivious to the fact that Sandro had played an equal part in every angle of each story. He spent long hours describing his and Sandro's adventures and the experiences they had shared, freely exploring and adventuring in the wild and hunting.

Sandro hung back, part of the group yet alone; while Andrew claimed all the limelight with his occasionally exaggerated tales of adventures in the wilds. Sandro hated feeling ignored and overlooked, and deplored Andrew's showiness. All of his life he had been Andrew's equal and best friend and now his perception was that he was somehow not good enough anymore. The more expressive and expansive Andrew became, the more withdrawn, unhappy, and even angry Sandro felt.

Andrew impressed Winifreda with his love of the land and vivid descriptions of the wildlife of Chile. He told of his long trek from the New York Estuary after arriving from Scotland, all the way to Chile working with his father, when he was a young boy. He described how they developed Casilla from nothing, and his adventures with Sandro as boys, and then as young men. He said not a word of the war!

His tales of the crossing of the Andes and their journey ultimately ending on their ranch in Buenos Aires District; were captivating. Her life had been so quiet and simple by comparison. Soon she thought she was in love. Meanwhile, he and Sandro worked well and made a good impression on Edward in the short time they spent together further developing the day-to-day operations.

However, Sandro became increasingly uncomfortable. His boyhood friend and latterly stalwart companion in manhood seemed to be working his way into ownership of the lovely ranch by way of weaving a spell around the young lady. Sandro disapproved, and felt threatened by the rumbles of change.

One evening, in their "digs" above the barn where rooms had been furnished for farm hands, an argument arose. Sandro accused Andrew of becoming a "social climber and womaniser". Andrew called Sandro an "undeveloped peasant". They had tasted Sangria in the company of the Cordners and unaccustomed to this, both heads had been affected. There were harsh words and a serious rift in their lifelong friendship appeared. From that time forward their relationship changed, and in the evenings when Andrew visited the homestead, Sandro stayed behind with the banjo he had acquired. He knew his place, he claimed. He preferred strumming to listening to the bragging. Occasionally Winifred thought she heard strains of the banjo but was too shy to go nearer and listen.

She was dazzled by Andrew Young McCormick and barely noticed that Sandro was less evident. Andrew who was hungry for family life, impetuously proposed and the twenty-nine-year-old Winifred Caroline Cordner eagerly accepted him. Edward was somewhat concerned about the changing family dynamics. He intuited a certain highly strung, possibly unstable element in Andrew's nature, but Winifred was determined.

The couple were married in a small and simple wedding, held in the Quilmes Church of all Saints, which Edward had caused to rise from the ground, and where Caroline was buried, on 21st April 1918. The blushing bride was very beautiful in white satin trimmed with lace, carrying the fashionably large cascading bouquet of white flowers. The groom wore a suit kindly loaned by Edward. Back at the estate, the wedding breakfast was shared by local Gauchos and "Mucho" women in bright skirts, with their guitars and lilting tango rhythms. All appeared to be well. It had been a whirlwind romance and these actions are often reconsidered later in life, with the onset of wisdom.

Andrew and Sandro had latterly been a good pair helping to manage the estate. Thus, Edward had no qualms when deciding to hand over the reins to his new son-in-law. He had heard all about the development of Casilla from the virgin wilderness, and felt a certain kinship with Andrew and Alexander's efforts since he had almost developed La Elvira from what had degenerated into something resembling wild country, himself.

Believing that with Andrew's experience, the ranch would be left in good hands, Edward Ellis Cordner answered the call to immigrate to Rhodesia to join his other younger daughter and her husband with their growing family; where he lived until his death. He had lost interest in La Elvira since it would never be inherited by Percy. Ultimately it would pass out of the Cordner name. In a way, he was a disappointed man who had dared much and yet not attained his dream.

His death on 24th September 1925, in Salisbury, Rhodesia; was caused by severe influenza and related heart failure. He was sixty-nine years old. Strangely the death certificate states that he was seventy.

Interestingly photographs show that the Irish Cordners had broad, strong facial features, fair, straw-coloured hair, high cheekbones, wide mouths and strong jawlines. Their body build was strong and muscular. The McCormicks on the other hand had softer facial features, and fair, ruddy-cheeked skin with the reddish-brown hair one associates with Scotland. The mixed genetics of the two families and their descendants bears a handsome blend.

As a de facto new master of the estate by marriage, Andrew's change of status further damaged his relationship with Sandro. However, Sandro chose to serve his friend and his wife. Left on the farm without the reassuring support of his recently acquired Father-in-law, Andrew felt insecure. Without the well-mannered, gentle, forthright leadership of a perceived "adoptive father" in Edward; things began to completely unravel for Andrew. It was all a little too much and too soon. The altered dynamics as a result of the marriage confused the relationships between Andrew, Sandro and Pedro. A storm began to develop on the not too far distant, emotional horizon.

It is significant to consider the impact on Andrew's life when as a very young boy he became an undersized young man working in partnership with Alexander; sharing trials, tribulations and responsibilities that were not normal for one so young. He had been separated from his twin and his mother. In an effort to make a late claim on manhood, he had rushed off to war only to discover to his chagrin that he was not a hero. He never told anyone the story of his capture, escape and desertion. He simply allowed people to assume he had been a war hero. It did not sit well on his conscience. He struggled in the face of his wife's admiration of what she assumed had been his bravery in the trenches. At night he dreamed of the war and occasionally got up and went walking out on the ranch to clear his head. Winifred waking to find herself alone did not know what to make of his moodiness. Wars affect marriage relationships.

Andrew and Winifred occupied the parental bed and Winifred was the lady of the house with a husband at the head of the table. In the intimacy of the new marriage Andrew and Winifred were poles apart with not much in common. Sandro though included at the table, felt embarrassed and unwilling to be there. He had been offered Percy's room and refused it. Eventually, he decided to simply "disappear" and return to his family in Chile. Feeling entitled after all their years together he helped himself to what he needed, and quietly left one day before dawn with Pronto bouncing along beside his master.

## Chapter Twenty-One
## McCormicks/Cordners/Cowpers

*"Our little lives are kept in equipoise By opposite attractions and desires, The struggle of the instinct that enjoys and the more noble instinct that aspires."*

*Longfellow – Haunted Houses*

Most sadly, Andrew was a scarred personality due to his fractured young life and many losses, separation from his twin sister, separation next from his mother and later from both his parents, his perceived lack of heroics and experiences in the war and finally the disappearance of his stalwart lifelong friend; he fell apart. He simply had no role model left to hold onto. Deprived of feminine influence his whole life, he had no idea how to interact with his new wife. Often, he took on moods and went walk-about for days, leaving Winifred all alone.

The short marriage was difficult and fraught with loud arguments. Perhaps he might have raised a hand to Winifred, we will never know for sure. Horrified by this development, Winifred decided to flee to safety in Rhodesia where her sister Emma, her husband Sydney, their children and her father were.

We can only guess how it might have been, and imagine this lone distraught woman hurriedly packing up and fleeing to Buenos Aires. She took the first available ship. During her sea voyage up the South American Coast, she realised that she was expecting a child. It was a dreadfully long journey interrupted by time spent in various ports en route, crossing the Atlantic in the becalmed doldrums from Buenos Aires, to Punto del Este, Rio Grande, Porto Belo, Rio de Janeiro, Jamestown, Walvis Bay, Luderitz; and finally; to Cape Town. Then from Cape Town to Durban by a British mail ship and afterwards by rail, eventually arriving in Salisbury after several days train journey.

All of this was endured during a pregnancy, which had been described by the ship's doctor as being a possible multiple birth. She knew that Andrew McCormick had a twin sister somewhere in America, who had been adopted into a Seventh-Day-Adventist family, so she was not surprised to have conceived twins. This was a delight, in truth; knowing that since she had left their father, the babies would at least have one another in childhood as they grew.

Andrew was likely off and about on his escapism activities and did not even notice her departure. It is difficult to conjecture whether, in the long run, he ever wondered what had happened. Did he even realise that it takes two to make a happy or an unhappy marriage?

Finally, a vastly pregnant Winifred stepped off the train in Salisbury falling into her father's welcoming arms, and was met by Emma and her little daughters Winifred and Patricia. Shortly afterwards on 17th July 1921, Winifred delivered twins, Ivor Ellis Cordner McCormick and Graham Austen Cordner McCormick. Could it be possible that somewhere in the vast outback of Argentina or Chile, Andrew ever learned that he was the father of twins?

On June 30th 1928, Andrew, possibly not aware of the divorce having been formalised in Glasgow, made the effort to free himself from the marriage in Buenos Aires; citing incompatibility and much argument. We know nothing more about the tragic Andrew Young McCormick. One can only imagine his suffering, and wonder, since there is no record of his death; if he had simply wandered off into the wilderness, became absorbed into an Amerindian tribe and eventually vanished. He may even have returned to Chile to look for his parents and effected a reconciliation. He may have ended his life running Casilla and even remarried, but this we will never know.

Evidence of the Cordner home farm no longer remains, and the house was not found when Cousin Graham visited Buenos Aires. The lovely little church is still there.

About sixty years later, it was confirmed by her son that Lillian McCormick, (Andrew's twin) had been taken in by the Seventh Day Adventist mission on Ellis Island. She grew within the mission environment and married a member of the church, ultimately settling in California. Her son Dr Anholm had become an orthodontic specialist, and travelled with the Seventh Day Adventist mission, to what had become Harare, Zimbabwe (formerly Salisbury, Rhodesia).

By chance, he cared for the orthodontics of Winifred Caroline Cordner McCormick's great-grandchildren, Patricia and Sean McCormick. Excited to encounter the McCormick name, he was very keen to connect with possible family relatives of his mother Lilian. This seems to suggest that he had succeeded in tracing Andrew's movements, and his marriage to Winifred Cordner, and possibly followed up enough to suppose that there may be a family remnant in Rhodesia based on Edward Cordner's journey there, after the marriage of Andrew and Winifred.

Sadly, Winifred's son Ivor Ellis Cordner McCormick was not willing to re-establish the family connection due to whatever had caused the breakdown of his parent's marriage; and forbade the younger generation from furthering the link. It seems that there had been some stories of violent interaction by Andrew toward Winifred. Of this tale of unacceptable behaviour, that the boys might have heard from their mother or their aunt, Ivor had never been able to forgive his father, whom he had never met. The oft-retelling of events that tends to also exaggerate a story is so very tragic, given that there was a lot of good reason to raise a sympathetic viewpoint.

One understands how threatened Winifred may have felt when Andrew flew into self-pitying rages and she never knew what might happen next. This gently raised woman had only known her aristocratic parents who exhibited contained softly-spoken mannerisms. Yet her stories of his childhood as told to her grandson suggest that as she aged, she understood what lay behind it all and had forgiven him. Possibly their stepfather, Sammy (Chevereux John Hasler) Samuels, was shocked by the story of Winifred's fleeing from Argentina, and harboured a personal image of a nasty person, rather than a war-ravaged man suffering from what is now known as Post Traumatic Stress Disorder.

Emma's husband Sydney was an architect as we know and one of his most well-known projects was the Salisbury Sports Club.

Winifred's teacher training and her status as a single mother encouraged her to seek work teaching, possibly after Edward passed away. She was engaged by an elderly Miss S.K. Darling her mother's younger friend who had trained as a teacher during the time when Caroline had been teaching young ladies in Dublin. Miss Darling was now a much older headmistress at Glengara Park, a school for young children in Dún Laoghaire, Dublin.

Happily, she sailed over to take up her teaching post with Ivor and Graham in tow. Emma followed with her twins Winifred and Patricia, and her younger daughters Elaine and Mary. The sisters undertook this journey, and spent several years in Dublin schooling their six little children with Winifred employed as a teacher at the school. We have no idea where they were accommodated but suspect it may have been in an inherited house on Merrion Close in Dún Laoghaire, which could have remained in the ownership of the Cordner family. Emma's youngest child Barclay stayed behind. Evidently, during that time, her marriage was floundering. While in Dublin, Winifred took the opportunity to travel across to Glasgow and formally divorce Andrew. The narrator's daughter Patricia visited the Glasgow registry years later, and found the divorce decree records.

Tales told by Ivor to his grandchildren of that time were laced with "derring-do" deeds. The two sisters had their hands full with six children to take care of. After four years in Dublin, as all the children grew, the damp sea air was diagnosed as being responsible for young Ivor's asthma which had become a problem. It was decided to return to the drier climate of Rhodesia with all the children. On board the ship, the sisters met "Sammy" Samuels who eventually married Winifred and helped her raise the McCormick twins to be the excellent young gentlemen they became.

Sammy Samuels is fondly remembered as a grandad by Hugh, Alan, Erica and Tamsin. He was somewhat older than Winifred but is still spoken of today as having been a rare gentleman, and his breeding and habits rubbed off on the younger generation. Photographs show him as a very handsome man surrounded by children and smoking a pipe. Latterly both Ivor and Graham indulged in pipe smoking as did Alan

Sydney Austen Cowper and Emma had five children, Winifred Cowper, Patricia Cowper, Elaine Cowper, Mary Cowper, and Barclay Sydney Austin Cowper. They were however later divorced. This occurred after her return to Rhodesia from Ireland. She later married Mr Shaw, who was a farmer/rancher with a large expanse of land in the lowlands of South Rhodesia near Beatrice.

Three of the daughters were fondly known as the triplets because Mary was very close in age to the twins and they all looked alike. As adults, the "triplets" went to live in the town of Victoria Falls. Emma's death certificate shows that she had suffered several illnesses: Anaemia, Secondary

Carcinoma, and Hypertension, with related failure of the right kidney. She was only fifty-nine years of age.

## Chapter Twenty-Two
## War Diaries

*"Be noble in every thought, and in every deed."*

*Longfellow – The Golden Legend*

In 2001 shortly after being dispossessed of his farm in Northern Zimbabwe, Alan the younger of Ivor's two sons travelled to Cape Town to visit his student son Sean who was busy qualifying for Civil Engineering. Sean's parents had dreams of him contracting worldwide and making a fortune, along with a name for himself. Alan's estranged wife was also in Cape Town. He had endured shocking trauma in Zimbabwe and therefore another reason for the visit was, for a period of rest and recovery, spending time with her.

He brought with him his late father's diaries. These were several worn-out journals written in faded pencil mostly, in an almost illegible scrawl; and he asked her to possibly create a family history for future generations.

There are three. One is dated 1939, another is dated 1943 and the third is dated 1944. These are painstakingly kept but clearly, the years 1940, 1941, and 1942 were not documented by him or at some stage they were lost or destroyed. This is a great pity. Alan had imagined that they would contain an unbroken record of his father's war years.

Given Ivor's personality and sense of humour, it was thought that these would make a fabulous story of the life of an R.A.F. "daredevil pilot" in North African Regiments detailing derring-do deeds during the extent of the war.

He flattered his lifelong friend and one-time wife with this comment: "You are very good with words, please turn Dad's diaries into a book." Twenty-one years passed by before she had the leisure in retirement to tackle the task. Alan's cousin showered her with his life's collection of documents, photographs and hand-drawn family trees. Many thanks to you, Graham Andrews.

An interesting detail on the front cover of Ivor's first diary is a note thus:
Miss E Cordner Casilla 26º Temuco Chile.
Another is Miss S.K. Darling Glengara Park, Dún Laoghaire Co. Dublin.

This raised two questions:
1. Did Emma plan to assist the twins in a possible plan to travel in search of their Scots father Andrew and his friend Sandro in Chile? It is more likely that she remembered the name at some point and informed Ivor. Ivor never followed up on this information.
2. Was Ivor planning on attempting to contact his Irish

relatives to learn more about his heritage? But we know now this possibly relates to the years at school in Dublin.

These two entries were invaluable in helping to build up the story of the McCormicks. At the time of starting this book, the narrator had no idea of them having been in Chile until a chance conversation with Alan, revealed that Winifred had entertained him with his grandfather's tales of exploring Chile and all the wildlife there.

Finally, one day, when she found herself with time on her hands, Solveig opened an old diary, and out fell a fine and faded old letter.

The postmark on the very well-worn aerogramme is Ceylon and the date is 14.11.43. The sender is Lieut. G.A McCormick (alias Bob); and the postmark is a field post office. The postage stamps are marked Ceylon to the value of 25 cents. She believes the head on the stamps to be that of young King George.

It is addressed to F/O I.E. McCormick, 123 Squadron, RAF, M.E.

The letter is marked as having been opened for censorship and then re-sealed.

What is astonishing is the beautiful style of the handwriting when one considers the conditions in which the letter was written.

The sender's address inside is 44 {U} K.A.R, Ceylon Command."

"Dear Ivor,

Your letter describing two smash-ups, of the 20.9.43 has just arrived, for which many thanks, but it is a hell of a time since I had any recent communication from you.

Is the second close shave going to be enough to keep you going for a while, or is there going to be one last supreme effort? Let me know and I'll send the flowers.

Whose fault was the second one though? Did you go to sleep? One of our drivers did the other day, with the result that he hit another truck; and I had to trundle two blokes into the nearest hospital. Well, all I hope; is that my body will be able to withstand as many bullets as yours has plane mishaps.

I appreciate your predicament concerning thieves. We had the same trouble in Mombasa and I would gladly have shot one, had I seen any. I was nearly shot myself one night; when slightly inebriated, 3 or 4 of us walked into the wrong tent.

Since last writing, we have moved right out into the bush with no civilians for miles, for which God be praised. The worst thieves are the monkeys which abound and the greatest menace are the numerous wild elephants. When we arrived at our "camp" (40 or 50 acres of thorn bush) all paths were strewn with elephant dung. Our only shelter is our groundsheet "bivvies" and a hastily pushed-up grass mess. We're only here to do some more bush training and then we go somewhere else – heaven knows where. I've only got with me 3 shirts, 3 pairs of shorts, a razor and a bed roll. So, I hope we will get a chance to recover some of our kits in the near future. Meanwhile, we have lots of work ahead of us and it can be as hot as hell here. I am getting thinner and all I want is a dose of fever and Dysentery combined to make me fade right away. I begin to have doubts about ever having a scrap and wish the bloody war was over. Are you in Rome yet? Don't be rude to the Pope when you see him and send me a picture postcard.

Cheerio and good luck.

Bob."

Another letter addressed to Winifred dated 8th September 1943; From the Air Vice Marshall reads simply that "80473 Pilot Officer I.E.C. McCormick is well and is with 237 Rhodesian Squadron"

Had she been concerned at not hearing from him and inquired at the Salisbury HQ?

Then another letter addressed to her dated 14th September 1943 reads:
Regarding 80473 Pilot Officer I.E.C. McCormick

It is with regret that I have to inform you that your son 80473 Pilot Officer Ivor Cordner McCormick was injured as a result of an aircraft accident at Bersisi on 31st August 1943. He is reported to be suffering from minor cuts and abrasions. No further details are available, but you may rest assured that, should any be received, the information will be conveyed to you immediately.

Signed by Air Vice Marshall – Commanding Rhodesian Air Training Group

It has been discovered that Bersisi is in Ethiopia. Perhaps this relates to the question from Bob about whether he was in Rome yet.

Ivor was the prankster and joker of the twins. Graham, also possessing a wonderfully dry sense of humour, was the quieter more reserved of the two. In Dublin, it was little Ivor who encouraged his brother to lie down between the tram tracks with him to see if they would fit under the tram when it came. Needless to say, the distraught mother and aunt were repossessed of the recalcitrant little boys by a man in a blue uniform and helmet. To the end of his life, Ivor loved to tell the tale of that day.

Old family photos show that Graham favoured his father's looks, and Ivor resembled his mother's family's features.

## Chapter Twenty-Three
## Ivor in Flight

*"Not in the clamour of the crowded street,
Not in the shouts and plaudits of the throng,
But in ourselves are triumph and defeat."*

*Longfellow – The Poet*

As an adult, Ivor loved flying. He could do anything with a light aircraft, if that is what you could call what was used in the second world war, in the North African and Middle Eastern Deserts.

Spitfires always remained his chief passion in life. And this aircraft also inspired a great sense of adventure in Alan.

When the second world war was brewing in Europe, Rhodesia, ever a brave and righteous country with a small pioneering population, busily building cities and industries and mining operations, boldly declared war against the German aggressor. Having done so, operations to train an Airforce worthy of becoming part of the R.A F began. Ivor McCormick, fondly known as Ivor the Driver in later years, appears to have enlisted in the war effort as a trainee pilot just before the New Year of January 1939. He was underage as many young men that enlisted were if all stories are to be believed.

Below is a piece of research drawn for some background

interest, also used to help the narrator understand the story being written.

"Godfrey Huggins, the Prime Minister of Southern Rhodesia (now Zimbabwe) from 1933 – 1953 became convinced that war was inevitable after the occupation of Czechoslovakia by Adolf Hitler's Nazi Germany in March 1939 and rearranged his Cabinet on a war footing. When Britain declared war on Germany on 3 September 1939, following the invasion of Poland, Southern Rhodesia issued its declaration of war almost immediately, and before any of the other Commonwealth Dominions.

The Commonwealth War Graves Commission (CWGC) does an outstanding job of commemorating those who lost their lives for their country and are buried in Zimbabwe. Their immaculately maintained cemeteries are in stark contrast to the disorder and chaos that characterises most of the municipal cemeteries. In the course of writing this article, photographs of every headstone at the CWGC cemeteries at Harare, Bulawayo and Gweru were taken.

On the outbreak of war in September 1939, the Government of Southern Rhodesia made an offer to the British Air Ministry to run a flying school and train personnel to man three squadrons (44, 237 and 266 (Rhodesia) Squadrons), which were duly accepted. The Rhodesian Air Training Group (RATG), operating from 1940–1945, was set up as part of the overall Commonwealth Air Training Plan. In

January 1940 the Government announced the creation of a Department of Air, completely separate from that of Defence and appointed Ernest Lucas Guest as Minister of Air. Guest inaugurated and administered what became the second-largest Empire Air Training Scheme, beginning with the establishment of three units at Salisbury, Bulawayo and Gwelo, each consisting of a preliminary and an advanced training school.

Rhodesia was the last of the Commonwealth countries to enter the Empire Air Training Scheme and the first to turn out fully qualified pilots. No. 25 Elementary Flying Training School at Belvedere, Salisbury opened on 24 May 1940. By August 1940, the schools could train up to 1800 pilots, 240 observers and 340 gunners per year. The original programme of an initial training wing and six schools was increased to 10 flying training schools and bombing, navigation and gunnery school and a school for the training of flying instructors as well as additional schools for bomb aimers, navigators and air gunners, including stations at Cranbourne (Salisbury), Norton, Gwelo and Heany (near Bulawayo). To relieve congestion at the air stations, six relief landing grounds for landing and take-off instruction and two air firing and bombing ranges were established. Two aircraft and engine repair and overhaul depots were set up as well as the Central Maintenance Unit to deal with bulk stores for the whole group.

The trainees came mainly from Great Britain but also from Australia, Canada, South Africa, New Zealand, the USA, Yugoslavia, Greece, France, Poland, Czechoslovakia, Kenya, Uganda, Tanganyika, Fiji and Malta. There were also pupils from the Royal Hellenic Air Force in training. Over 7,600 pilots and 2,300 navigators were trained by the RATG during the war.

We know already that Southern Rhodesia was the first Commonwealth country to declare war on Germany after Hitler marched on Czechoslovakia. A brave little, very young country that Rhodesia was at the time; threw herself into war preparations in early 1939. How it came about that Ivor enlisted before the official declaration, may have occurred because, in a small community, there might already have been stories of war involvement; and preparations had begun before the official declaration by the Prime Minister.

In hangars on three airfields, namely Salisbury, Thornhill and Gwelo the rebuilding and repairing of largely privately owned erstwhile WW1 craft began. Ivor joined up immediately even though he was not quite old enough to enlist. His first year of training was largely focused on mechanics, with fairly regular flying school trips, training on radio coding, and early radar training as well as map reading, although he was taken on several training flights between the various airfields. He experienced training flights to Bulawayo almost daily as they were moving equipment around and dropping off supplies as they became available. Mostly on afternoons after those flights, he swam. He records with relish his purchase of "khakis" as a uniform of sorts. After some time, he was allowed to fly with a qualified instructor, and the heady experience of being airborne captured him for life. Reading his diaries though reveals that it was not all work, there was also plenty of time for play, and those were happy days.

There is an entry about Ivor flying from Salisbury to Bulawayo and back before breakfast in a YAV There is also mention of him piloting, but possibly not solo, a YAV Douglas Aircraft. All efforts to discover more about this craft have only revealed that it was an early edition single-engine aircraft originally built for private use by the company that is now Boeing. Most of the rest of the week involved flight school.

He spends routine time in stores and mechanics. It is difficult to tell whether all the comments about flight school are referring to classroom work or actual aircraft familiarisation activities. It seems that he spent a lot of time handling and sorting parts of aircraft. It is noted that there was quite a lot of effort put in by many volunteers, to help reassemble old, damaged WW 1 craft; for use with the training of the early enlistees.

On Saturday 21st January he notes that he went up with a person called Hales in "BP" over PE. It is assumed this was referring to the plane and a short flight over Prince Edward School Area. The **Boulton Paul Defiant** is a British interceptor aircraft that served with the Royal Air Force (RAF) during World War II. The Defiant was designed and built by Boulton Paul Aircraft as a "turret fighter", without any fixed forward-firing guns, also found in the Blackburn Roc of the Royal Navy.

On Monday 23rd January, he mentions test-flying a VP-YAR This appears from research to be a craft capable of landing and taking off from water.

This was a test flight after the plane had been standing for three and a half years. The narrator's curiosity is so aroused. She mentions at this point; that she is fascinated by aircraft and loves flying. The sensation of lifting from the ground is exceptionally thrilling. She almost wishes that she had lived in that time and space, sharing Ivor's delight in what he was doing.

On Tuesday 24th January he mentions packing instruments for repairs to S. Smithson's "The Duke's" Stenson, ZS-ADX and Fairchild ZS-AMM in a hangar for the night. It is amazing what a variety of aircraft was available to the early Southern Rhodesian Aircrew all those years ago.

The diary continues with a similar daily routine.

For the sake of history, it is worth noting that Graham alias Bob; started work at Shell Company on February 1st. Also on that day, Ivor took up residence in a room rented from a Mrs Seddon.

As we know, Ivor loved swimming and recorded his long hours of training at the city baths. He was also a keen ballroom dancer and records many tea dances with a lady called Wyn. He regularly met up with his mother and his brother Graham who at the time was fondly known as Bob. He records his first solo flight with great excitement and shortly after this, he and several others were to be awarded their Wings. He describes with relish the purchase of his "Blues" for the event. A qualified pilot is automatically an officer, being called a Flight Officer. He describes with pride being able to use the Officers Mess and quite naturally the head-turning effect of his "blues" when he was "out and about" in town.

An interesting piece of information is that when the Home Office in England learned of the Airforce training activities in Rhodesia, it was decided to move the RAF training from Northern England to Rhodesia where there was less danger from the incessant bombing raids by Germany. At that point, many good aircraft and pilot trainers arrived and the whole operation became much more sophisticated and exciting. This is already mentioned above in the piece of research information that is shared.

As the young Flight Officers received their Wings, they were sent to Durban to await transfer to Aden for further operations training. Ivor describes his train Journey with delight. From Salisbury through Gwelo to Bulawayo, Francistown to Mafikeng, Johannesburg, Pietermaritzburg and ultimately Durban. He waxes lyrical about the last stretch coming into Durban as the track winds through the hills back and forth laboriously through stunning forested gorges with rivers below.

Peculiarly the forces camp at Natal Command in Durban was held in some disdain by the Rhodesians. Perhaps it had only recently been developed and South Africa as a nation was not fully committed to the war at that time. The RAF chaps that were gathered from all the other commonwealth countries, looked with some disdain at the South African Camp and the lack of discipline among the South African men. The only redeeming factors were the lovely beaches and for Ivor, his daily swims were a delight.

The delay was interminable and they all became bored and irritable, anxious to travel North and get some of the action. But this long wait was broken by his wonderful mother boarding the train and coming all the way to see him before his time for departure arrived. They enjoyed Durban together visiting the Playhouse, a theatre venue which also showed grainy black and white moving pictures at the start of which, all stood to sing "God Save the King" before The Pathe News began. They also occasionally took tea at the Edward Hotel, a gracious establishment on the beachfront, and just generally passed quality time together. Possibly the wonderful National History Museum near to the City Hall and the Cenotaph was a destination.

## Chapter Twenty-Four
## Action

*"In character, in manners, in style in all things,
the supreme excellence is simplicity."*

Longfellow - Kavanagh

Finally, the great day arrived and they boarded several troop ships that were to travel in convoy up Africa's Eastern coasts through Aden in Yemen and eventually through Suez which was most eagerly anticipated by them all. The diary describes the days on board the ship; the broiling heat during the day, the cold at night, the daytime sunbathing and above all the beautiful deep seas and dark skies at night, spangled by bright stars. There were times when dolphins accompanied the ships leaping just ahead and to the side of the bows as if showing the way. Ivor doesn't mention this but the author's father who also sailed North, spoke fondly of Gracie Fields singing to the troops on the decks before the ship sailed out of Durban's harbour.

They paused long in Mombasa waiting for a further convoy. It is not known where the other ships forming the convoy were expected to come from but possibly one or two were from India and Ceylon, perhaps from Australia and New Zealand, or even another from Durban. The young men enjoyed the port and its environment, and some of them, having received passes, crossed to Zanzibar. It is well known that this historic island is loaded with architectural treasures and the ancient Arabic culture is alluring. Loads of little shops in narrow streets are a foretaste of Middle Eastern cultures. Many varieties of delicately crafted, beautiful silver jewellery, and decoratively cast and styled brass works, are on view for sale to tourists. Ancient carved doors to homes in winding alleyways are an art exhibition in themselves. And then, of course, there are beautiful beaches in Mombasa and surrounding the exotic Zanzibar Island.

At last, the rest of the convoy arrived, docked and took on fuel and supplies. They set sail again and as they travelled North, excitement mounted. Many were keen to see the famous Suez Canal. But this was not yet to be. They were informed that there was further training at an unnamed place, inland of Aden. However, Aden is famed for its beauty with the harbour framed by Basalt mountains, and the sight of exotic Dhows darting around. Anticipation continued to mount among the young men.

Finally, they were in Aden and troop carriers arrived to carry them to a camp in the desert. Here further months of flight training and desert warfare continued. They were all so disappointed by the delay of the anticipated trip through Suez. Gradually the grimness of what they were preparing for began to sink in. Life in the desert is an extreme one. Hot in sunlight and cold in the dark. Night falls suddenly and in the absence of geophysical points of reference, it is easy to lose oneself, so it's unwise to go walkabout. Barracks were basic and food was not that great but adequate. In this part of the diary, Ivor mentions his training in towing up and releasing gliders. The desert updrafts were useful for this. The narrator is curious as to how and where the use of gliders occurred in the war activities. It occurs now that since they were not engine-powered craft, their silent flights may have been useful for espionage purposes.

Eventually, they set sail again and passed through the long-awaited Suez Canal, a one-hundred-mile-long canal dug between two lakes and joining the Red Sea to the Mediterranean; finally docking in Alexandria. They were directed to desert camps and airfields and assigned duties and barracks. Superior Officers briefed them on the current war situation and battle tactics. Suddenly the whole adventure became serious. At this point, apart from descriptions of various after-hours activities, there were several trips abroad to find a bottle of whiskey, associated pranks in barracks, and card playing. Nothing is written about operational activities.

It is assumed that he would be sent on "business" sorties of unnamed nature, be it surveying what was on the ground, dropping a paratrooper or two, or something else more incendiary. He does mention a trip to the Negev desert and being impressed by Mount Sinai. On that trip, he was returning solo and records being delighted with having rolled the plane wing over wing a couple of times and attempting a rather dangerous full circle in the air. He told the tale so nothing went amiss.

Once his various missions were accomplished, and he was alone in the aircraft; the joys of spring would inspire him and he could not resist some aerobatics. On a couple of occasions, he passed too close to a dune and damaged his plane somewhat. Ivor could never resist testing his capabilities with the various aircraft he was flying during the war, in the British Colonies of North Africa.

We know from his brother's letter that twice he experienced mishaps, damaging both the aircraft and himself. Perhaps he drew enemy fire to save a fellow pilot, we do not know, but it would be the sort of thing he was capable of. Possibly on another occasion he misjudged a dune and made an awkward landing that damaged the belly and undercarriage of the craft. He is no longer with us and we can only guess. His whole life was pushed to the limits. A courageous and honourable man, with an impossibly infectious and playful sense of humour, added to a very handsome face atop a broad, fit and wiry frame, made him irresistible. He played all manner of tricks and made children laugh uproariously at his silliness, and spent hours playing Solitaire. He was full of pranks and teasing, but through it all, he was an extremely kind and gentle person. His sincerity could not be equalled!

This was his light-hearted description of events: "As a result of my antics in the air in North Africa, I was ultimately sent home. The RAF valued their aircraft, and said I was having too much fun with them."

Thus, we reach the point when the 1943 diary describes young Ivor as confined to barracks. It was January. We have no idea why. Was it as he said because he had a couple or a few too many accidents when flying? Even his confinement to barracks is detailed in his diary as an apparent party. There he gathered life-long friendships and together he and his mates made the best of a difficult situation during an extremely cold desert winter, where the icy wind blows incessantly, in makeshift barracks. The man who had started life as an asthmatic child suffered several bouts of feverish flu, even possibly pneumonia. It seems there were not enough blankets and poor rations. At the time the war was stretching on and on depressingly, and Britain was devastated. Food supplies and clothing, blankets, medicine and other comforts were very much in short supply. It could not have been at all comfortable for any flight officer facing court-martial. The detention went on for several months.

His diary tells in long day-to-day detail of his time confined to barracks awaiting court-martial. He seems to have spent weeks at a time reading one book after another. It was a bitter winter and he was very sick with flu that would not budge. Blankets were not plentiful but a person he calls "Doc" loaned him an overcoat to put over his blanket. "Doc" features largely. There were a couple of high-jinks with the men getting out somewhere to cadge drinks and pies. Then the weather improved and he improved and was able to get out and take some exercise. The men also seemed to play cards an awful lot.

The incredibly long wait for the expected court martial was difficult to endure. One by one his mates that were "Confined to Barracks" with him, stood before the court-martial. Some were released and went back to their regiments but others did not. It was almost a case of "spin the bottle".

Curiously there are letters to his mother indicating that he had been active, during this time and had been in an accident while flying but was not hurt. Therefore, it suggests that he had been one of those released to continue service. We understand that he had been able to fly during that year but had never mentioned it in the diary. At this point of the story, it occurs to the narrator that perhaps the three missing diaries were confiscated by his Officer in Charge, suspicious of what had been recorded regarding Ivor's activities. Was his journaling considered to be a fault? Who knows? Ivor's character was unassailable. He would never have knowingly breached any codes of conduct. If by chance he wrote something in his diary about anything in his wartime activities, it is certain that at the time it was completely innocent and never once considered by him to be of any interest to anyone but himself.

We will never know what happened to those diaries. Perhaps they were simply lost in transmission or even, never written at all. There is a huge question mark about his interrupted confinement to barracks that we will never have an answer for.

The cold winter and sickness passed and the hot weather bored down on the camp. Time marched on relentlessly and another cold winter arrived. Ultimately his day dawned and he was called to account, for what we do not know. As he put it in his diary; on a "Monday morning in early January 1944, I was relieved of His Majesty's Service." Shortly afterwards he boarded a ship at Suez, bound via Aden, then Mombasa to Durban, A sad return journey of the one he had taken in high spirits with his buddies, heading out to the great war adventure. As pilots, they were "Flight Officers" and enjoyed many comforts that other servicemen did not. They enjoyed wearing their "blues" to dinner and special events, as well as disembarking thus attired, at various ports en route.

This time around, however, it was different. He was once again a private individual. As the ship was delayed in Mombasa harbour, Ivor began to ponder what on earth to do next with his life. He dreamily watched port activity, sat in port-side bars drinking tea, and thought long and hard about what might have been, how his discharge may have saved his life and how valuable simply being alive was. Those days in Mombasa thinking things through may have been a dramatic period of personal growth and maturity of spirit. His viewpoint on life became philosophical. We can say he grew up there.

He remembered stories his mother told him of life in Argentina and how his father had been a Scottish farmer's son in Chile, who had arrived on the Cordner ranch one day with his friend Sandro, looking for work as cowboys. This seemed to Ivor to be incredibly romantic and adventurous. He dreamed of days in the saddle, free of all routine and bullying.

By the time the ship left Mombasa, he had forwarded a letter to his mother asking her to suggest he go to work on his aunt's farm in Beatrice when he eventually arrived back in Rhodesia. But of course, the journey home was long and arduous. While in Durban he had the forethought to open a bank account which would later stand him in good stead. He deposited a good portion of his British severance pay and boarded a train for the long journey North, then West, then East again to Johannesburg, North West through the Northern Cape to Botswana and then Bulawayo. There he disembarked and hitch-hiked Southwards towards Beatrice and Gowerlands Estate.

His diary continues with his having to use his mechanical capabilities to fix pumps for house and barn water supplies and correct windmill abilities to move as required in different wind directions and speeds. He repaired miles and miles of fencing and never mounted a horse. He fed the cattle and trekked around on a rickety bicycle. The disappointment of the punctured dream bubble of himself galloping around in wild west style rises from the pages of his diary. But eventually, he was allowed to use an old nag and teach himself to ride. After a time, he was a good rider and graduated to more spirited animals which made his life out under the Rhodesian sun, a life of adventure as well as hard work. At least he was later able to claim to have been a cowboy. This impressed his future daughter-in-law more than he ever knew.

As on the farm in Chile, a Rhodesian farm, particularly in the deep south bordering the great Limpopo River also attracted wildlife. Ivor, having grown up in Rhodesia was no doubt well acquainted with African animals. Wildlife appeared on farmlands. The distinctively marked Wild Dogs, with swishing tails and large alert ears, better known as Lycaon Pictus or Painted Wolves, were endemic. Leopards were attracted to beef farms where young calves were easy prey. Vervet Monkeys and Baboons roomed freely attracted to ripening Maize and domestic vegetable gardens and orchards. Grazing antelope such as Waterbuck and Kudu leapt easily over fences, and Warthog was a favourite food source for the indigenous African farmhands.

Thus Ivor, and likely Graham too, had a deep love for wild Africa and her inhabitants. The grasslands teemed with gazelles known as Impala while statuesque Kudus with their magnificent horns, were always gazed at in awe. Then there were the Cats; Lions, and Cheetah, which are the fastest animals, though only over a limited distance. There were also Leopards with their magnificent spotted fur, so sought after by fashion furriers, the night hunters one seldom sees in daylight unless particularly blessed. Snakes of many kinds kept one aware when out walking and encouraged people to wear tall boots.

He had not heard from Graham since the letter quoted here earlier. Then on 5th October 1944, he received a most polite and respectful telegram informing him of Graham's honourable decease. His presence was required in Salisbury by his family. What a spear to the heart shock this was!

The telegram reads thus:

Addressed to: I. McCormick Esq.,
Stamped by: B.S.A. Police date 5 October 1944

Sir,

It is with deep regret, that I have to inform you that your brother, Bob, has been killed in action. Your people desire that you come to Salisbury as soon as possible.

Please accept the deepest sympathy from myself and the members of this police detachment.

I have the honour to be,

Sir,

Your obedient servant, KR Howard 1/Sgt. Member 1/c Beatrice


Ivor returned to Salisbury to be with his grief-stricken mother and stepfather and no doubt; his aunt Emma and her family also travelled to Salisbury in sympathy.

McCormick men internalize difficult experiences. There are no descriptions of grief and funeral. There is a photograph of a grave. The narrator is confident that Graham's posthumous medals were honourably returned to his mother. The next entry in the diary is in large, childlike lettering scrawled across the page:

"MOMMY GONE AWAY."

"Mom on holiday."

From this, it is easy to recognise that grief-stricken Ivor is not coping as well with the loss of his twin as others thought he might. The narrator suspects that a "getaway" and "change of scene", were diagnosed to help Winifred cope with the devastating news. Perhaps it was assumed that a WWII veteran was perfectly able to cope with his grief, but not so.

### Chapter Twenty-Five
### Graham

*"No endeavour is in vain. Its reward is in the doing;
And the rapture of pursuing
Is the prize the vanquished gain."*

*Longfellow – The wind over the chimney*

Below is a copy of a news report regarding Graham Austen's bravery in Burma.

Tuesday, November 21 1944

THE EAST AFRICAN STANDARD…………………………………PAGE THREE

# The Bunker Battle
## TWO COMPANIES CAPTURE A STRONG POSITION
(From our War Correspondent, G. KINNEAR)

*(COPYRIGHT).* *Yazagyo Burma -*
Yazagyo Village in Kale Township - Yazagyo is the northernmost village in Kale Township, Kale District, of western Burma. The Yazagyo Airfield, where the US 965th and 966th Airborne Air Control Squadrons were stationed during World War II, is located 3 kilometres north of the town.

**Chauk –** incidental piece of interest - Chauk is a town and river port in Magway Region, north-central

Myanmar, on the Irrawaddy River. It is located across the river from Seikphyu and is connected by a bridge. Here the British had discovered oil and built oil fields and a refinery in 1902. - Possible interest in holding Burma? – Research Battle of Yenaungyaung.

*On the morning of September 26$^{th}$ 1944, two companies of a Nyasaland unit were serving with the East African forces in the first serious attack of the advance down the road to Kalemyo. I have already described in an earlier article the adventures of two other companies – one Nyasa and the other Uganda – which went two miles round the rear to beat up the road towards the main Japanese positions but were prevented from doing so by a thunderstorm which flooded the Chaung and cut them off on the wrong side of the stream so that they were unable to carry out the whole of their original plan. But they killed a dozen Japanese and captured one. Their own casualties were nil.*

*The main attack was carried out by one company, commanded by Major Terence McGuire, and the plan provided that a platoon from the remaining elements of the Nyasaland unit would give covering fire.*

*The Japanese Bunker or bunkers were a big built-up position on both sides of the main road with communicating passages underneath the road itself, and an interlocking system of trenches, firing points and so on. The company attack was to be made from the right-hand side of the road while the platoon would provide its covering fire from the left-hand side; with plenty of mortar bombs.*

*When the right-hand defences had been seized, the covering fire from the platoon would cease and the attacking company would cross the road and attack the Japanese positions on the left.*

*So, at first light on September 26$^{th}$, that is to say, about half-past five, the attacking force moved from its base and, after covering three-quarters of a mile of road, dumped its packs on a pimple (?) by the roadside.*

*Then the Nyasas went forward, carrying picks and shovels as well as their weapons so that they could dig themselves in if necessary. The covering platoon went on also to await the noise of firing, which would be their signal to open up.*

*The attacking Company did a compass march two miles through the bush and came out near the road about half a mile behind the Japanese bunkers. Two African scouts were sent ahead to report back the moment they saw enemy movement. The Company moved quietly ahead in Platoons through the forest about a hundred yards off the road. After going about three hundred yards the two scouts came back with a report that they had seen a Japanese sentry standing on the bunker on the spot which was the Company's first objective.*

### Tree-Dodging

*The leading platoon commanded by Lieutenant Graham McCormick from Southern Rhodesia was deployed immediately and slowly advanced in very open formation dodging from tree to tree. The Japanese had thinned out the undergrowth all around their defences and visibility was between 150 and 200 yards, which is pretty far in the forest. Large numbers of trees had been cut down to make the bunkers and the cover the Nyasas expected to find was not there.*

*McCormick advanced to within a hundred yards of the Japanese without being spotted, and then he opened up on the sentry who however was only wounded and got back into the bunker. He was killed later. A machine gun then began to fire on McCormick's left section and it was pinned down for a time but then stealthily crawled to within about thirty yards of the enemy and then threw in a shower of grenades. Eight Japanese were seen to run out of the rear of the defences on the other side of the road and McCormick sent his reserve section across to try to cut them off. One was hit and wounded but he got away.*

*Then McCormick's platoon assaulted their objective with all three sections. In a very spirited attack, which there was no stopping, they went slap through the Japanese positions and across the top and chased out onto the road and there killed four of them. The askaris came streaking across the open grassy space with their bayonets in the face of the Japanese machine-gun fire and they simply swarmed over the position, clearing it out with grenades.*

*But the success was gained at a price. Lieutenant Graham McCormick and his African platoon sergeant beside him were both shot by a Japanese sniper from around the back of the bunker. The sergeant was killed outright. McCormick was carried back to his unit headquarters and died there shortly afterwards.*

*In civil life, McCormick was a public servant in Rhodesia and his home town is Salisbury. Both men were shot at about ten yards range from across the road. The Japanese sniper tried to escape but was killed immediately by infuriated Nyasas, whose blood was up. Meanwhile the platoon behind not stopping; were mopping up in pairs. One man with a bayonet fixed put a few rounds of rifle fire into the enemy position and then his mate threw in a grenade or two.*

**Drawing Enemy Fire**

*The Japanese were caught by surprise. It was found later that only one section had occupied the portion of the defences which were our first objective, some thirty others having been drawn over to the positions across the road by the fire of the covering platoon. That platoon certainly did their stuff gallantly. They ran around in the open to draw*

Japanese fire and made as much noise as possible to give their comrades on the main job the maximum opportunity.

Back in the area of conflict the mopping up went on. Four more Japanese found cowering terror-stricken in bunkers were killed. They were too frightened to fire. One of them took refuge right in the middle of the communication tunnel under the road and the job of getting him out took an hour. Though several attempts were made to dispose of him by grenades, the distance was too great and the angle too difficult. Nobody could go along a trench without risk of being killed so a hole was dug into it from the road above and then a grenade did the job.

Liaison was made with the covering platoon and another series of bunker positions was found across a thirty-foot-wide creek on the Chaung, where the stream was in full flood. Two platoons went past in full view of the firing slits but the bunkers were empty. Having secured the whole of the communication system, the Company proceeded to deal with the second objective – the defences on the left of the road – but found that the Japanese had left hurriedly and in confusion. Food, cooking utensils and clothing were scattered about. At one o'clock in the afternoon, the whole Company gathered in the middle of the captured enemy system and made a firm base. It was estimated that the total enemy strength was probably about thirty-five. Twelve were known to have been killed and an unknown number wounded. Most of the Japanese weapons – grenade dischargers, machine guns of various calibres and rifles were captured.

*Point of last resistance under construction*

*Japanese bunker funnel firing slit.*

### Japanese Bunkers

*You may be interested to know something about what a Japanese "bunker" is like. The positions taken by us at Yazagyo were a very good example of these extraordinarily strong defensive earthworks and were of course of some age and made at a time when the Japanese hold on Burma had not been seriously challenged and they had ample time to prepare a strong line on a carefully planned basis. The bunker itself is a room in which one can stand upright and it is reinforced with heavy logs around the sides and the ceiling. For the most part, each bunker – a position usually consists of several – has one or two firing slits. The slit is funnel-shaped, tapering to the inside where it is only about four inches wide so that while the defender with a rifle or machinegun has a wide field of fire and vision, the slit cannot be fired into except at close range, and it is very difficult indeed to put a grenade into from more than a few yards away.*

*In a map of this particular position which was found, there were "centres of the last resistance'. These suicide chambers are usually at the junction of two or more communication trenches and under pressure the Japanese fall back into them when the bunkers and outer defences are lost. The suicide chambers where the last stand is made are windowless, are logged with tree trunks like the main bunkers and have tons of earth on top. In the Yazagyo position, taken at a such small cost, there were in all some twenty bunkers astride the road, the whole being some three hundred yards in-depth, and across the Chaung there was another row of bunker positions of some similar length.*

*There was a primitive warning system made from tins filled with stones hung on wires leading to section commanders' quarters and as far as could be seen, the Japanese had never come out of the perimeter once they were inside.*

*The general view is that we took the enemy by surprise as they were preparing to garrison the defences in force and that only a small advance party had arrived. The plan of the bunkers indicated that when fully defended, the Japanese armament would include a very considerable number of light and medium machine guns and also anti-tank weapons. Had these bunkers been defended by their full complement, it may well have taken a full brigade operation to have captured them and the price paid would have been high. The point can be made, too, that as we came upon these positions accidentally, and decided to attack them at once, the troops did not have the benefit of softening up by air assault.*

Memorial

## Chapter Twenty-Six
## Ivor the Driver

*"A man of such genial mood*
*The heart of all things, he embraced."*

Longfellow – Prelude to Tales of a Wayside Inn.

As the narrator knew him, Ivor was a wise and gentle, kindly father and ultimately Father-in-law, a good friend, and a fabulous babysitter when needed At one time he was a financial advisor, and at another, he was in air traffic control at the national airport in Salisbury, which occasionally featured an elephant wandering onto the runway. This may have been exciting for onlookers, but not so for the captain, crew and air traffic control. He led a varied and interesting life, this very talented man. When he took early retirement, he applied himself to long-distance study to qualify as a Fellow of the Chartered Institute of Secretaries. How utterly impressive! He managed his finances quietly without fuss or discussion, never seeming to deprive himself but always living a simple life, he devised ways to provide for all his family more than adequately.

After the war, his next airborne hobby was towing gliders into the air until they caught an updraft, before releasing the catch to free them; at the local gliding club. He just loved the challenge. Many a glider pilot remembers him fondly. Later he became the all-time favourite pilot at the parachute club. He developed a technique of ascending and descending in steep, dizzying, stomach-dislodging spirals. According to him, this saved time, fuel and airspace; but possibly also increased his thrill factor.

So that was how he became known as Ivor the driver.

He had a talent for fixing and inventing all sorts of mechanicals. In his backyard, he had a comprehensive workshop, where he spent countless hours tinkering. This was likely why his two sons became so handy with mechanicals. Thus, he also became dubbed "Ivor McGyver". Does anyone remember the entertaining television series about McGyver, the talented young man who could invent a solution for any difficult situation he found himself in? That's our Ivor.

Ivor the Driver met a group of British Airways captains who had been training pilots in a North African country. They had heard of the perfect hot-air balloon conditions in the area where Ivor lived. His reputation had reached them, and they invited him for a drink or two. The upshot of that was that he volunteered his farming son Alan's eight-ton vehicle, to transport the baskets and balloons.

Consequently, the whole family became involved in a ballooning escapade. These were Ivor, his son, his daughter-in-law; a friend of hers Solvej from the Danish Embassy, and their two young children. On a cold winter morning just before dawn, everyone assembled at an open field. The pilots all wore shirts with captions on their backs: "We achieve more before breakfast than you do in a day".

The rising sun shining through the gradually inflating balloons was an unforgettable sight. The hiss and pop of the gas burner's inflation, and then the excitement, as the balloons gradually erected themselves. There followed the straining to hold the basket on the ground as one by one the passengers climbed in. The family members were surprised and thrilled to be included in the jaunt. Then began the gentle ascent as the controlled flame heat, was slowly increased into the balloon. The soft morning breeze carried them along as they continued to climb. The most magical part of the experience is that when you are wind-borne, you are not wind-blown. It's an interesting sensation moving in the wind with not a hair on the head being disturbed.

The brightly coloured balloons drifted along in the peace of the morning above the trees, sleeping farms and glistening dams, where cattle hunkered down in repose.

Eventually, the gas volume decreased and they started to drift towards the ground. The pilots prepared the passengers for managing the jolt of the landing basket. Suddenly an unexpectedly strong gust of wind, blew them over a hedge away from the planned landing site, into a large field inhabited by beautiful horses. These in turn took fright and went galloping away, trying to escape the moving balloon shadow; which seemed to be chasing them. The flight had gone off the predicted course. The vehicles that had been following for retrieval purposes could not reach the landed craft. As they descended, it became obvious that the startled horses were all in foal and were definitely very finely bred.

They jolted to the ground and carefully, quietly clambered out, beginning immediately to collect, fold and pack the deflated balloon. Nobody breathed a word as they were aware of the trespass, and did not want to further startle the horses. Actually; the horses stopped fleeing, and turned back towards the group, ears alert, curious to discover what they were. Never underestimate a pregnant thoroughbred's intelligence and innate curiosity.

Whereupon a farm truck arrived, driven by a very angry farmer brandishing a rifle, and threatening to sue for the full value of any lost, treasured, unborn foals!

So, the morning did not end very well.

That evening they all met for dinner at Alan's city home. It was a jovial meal full of amusing tales of escapades in hotels around the world between flights. The funniest of all was about the one pilot who on returning home to Heathrow, was identified at customs by a sniffer dog. His bag was duly opened to reveal that, the very hung-over gentleman had packed his full, untouched, English-breakfast-tray; in his suitcase! Fortunately, he and his pals had been passengers on the flight.

The most convivial evening ended with a plan to celebrate the irrepressible Ivor-the-Driver's seventieth birthday, by taking him up high enough in a balloon; that he could clamber out, and parachute down. Gasp!

A little crowd of friends and family gathered at the site to watch the event, holding their hearts in their mouths.

He landed safely amid uproarious shouts and applause.

## Chapter Twenty-Seven
### Ivor and Sue

*"It is a characteristic trait of a great and liberal mind that it recognises humanity in all its forms and conditions."*

*Longfellow - Hyperion*

After the death of Graham and his return to Salisbury from "Gowerlands Estates", Ivor needed to re-invent himself in a post-war situation when the war was not yet over. To keep himself occupied he accepted work with "The Old Mutual" and started selling insurance policies. Surely his winning personality made him successful in this task. In those days salesmen went door to door and plied their sales pitches. Many a door was slammed in their faces but persistence paid. That is just how it was done back then.

One day a door was opened by a most beautiful young girl with a magnificently, glorious mane of thick mahogany curls tied back from her face. She was wearing a simple gingham dress, a shirt-waister with frilled detail. His heart literally stopped and he knew he was in love. Sadly, she did not want an insurance policy. She was an aspirant bookkeeper and was busy with her studies, conscientiously studying and balancing her ledgers and journals. He didn't get past the door.

Delirious with the image of this lovely girl his feet drew him back to that door day after day until she allowed him to come in and poured him some tea.

He learned that her grandparents the Hoffmans had escaped from The Orange Free State, in South Africa, and had trekked into Rhodesia looking for some good land to settle on. In the southern region of Rhodesia, there is a little town called Enkeldoorn where some Boers escaped from colonial harassment, and even today most still speak Afrikaans. In time past, the Dutch language had evolved, or become desiccated, into what their British "Masters" termed Kitchen Dutch. The Boers saw it as a fresh independent language in keeping with their new life in Africa. Enkeldoorn means "single thorn".

Josias Philip Hoffman, commonly known as Sias Hoffman (1807 – 1879) was a South African Boer statesman and was a chairman of the provisional government of the Orange Free State which had been claimed by the settlers in the name of the reigning Prince, William III, in the House of Orange-Nassau Principality. It was a declaration of independence in the face of the British overlords whose presence they took exception to. That Principality originally in the North of France, and latterly part of the Southern Netherlands, was the scene of religious oppression of

Protestants, and many fled to South Africa and are now known as Huguenots.

Sias Hoffman served as temporary President in the Orange Free State but was relieved of his position after only one year in office when it came to light that he had supplied gunpowder to the Basotho tribes in sympathy with their struggle against the BSAP and associated mercenaries in the battle for British dominion in the southern regions of Africa. Hoffman's descendants may have been dispossessed of their farm Slootkraal in the Wepener District of the Orange Free State due to the gunpowder kegs incident, and they decided to trek north into Rhodesia.

All of this is unclear, but one of the Hoffman daughters ultimately married a Naude. According to tradition; it seems a wheel of one of the Hoffman trek wagons broke, and they had to camp where they were. This led to the building of a little house and the planting of vegetables. Ultimately, that is where they stayed. From being a fairly important and well-to-do family in the Free State of Orange, they became humble settlers in Manicaland, Southern Rhodesia. Far from any town, the business of survival became very much hand-to-mouth. But being of proud descent and experienced farmers, they thrived.

Now the daughter who married Jean Phillipe Naudé did so because it is a proud name of Huguenot origin. They left the family home farm and started a farm of their own. Jacoba Marianna Hoffman Naudé bore six or seven children. One was Susannah Jacoba Naudé who grew up to be the bewitchingly beautiful girl that captured Ivor's heart at first sight. They were dirt poor and it seems that Pappa Naudé preferred the wine bottle to other refreshments. He was a violent man. Susannah's recollections of her young life were miserable.

The children were barefoot and their clothes, sometimes sewed from flour sack cotton, were recycled, patched, ragged and faded. They had to walk far on their little bare feet to the local farm school. Susannah liked to tell people that she managed to get her first pair of shoes at the age of sixteen. She had been working in the village and started to acquire her simple clothing, as well as sewing her cotton dresses.

There was a famously well-known barefoot priest (Prester John?) in the district whose reputation has outlived the memory of his name. And it was he who recognised Susannah's innate refinement, intelligence and talent. He arranged for her to go to Salisbury where she found work in an office and attended evening college to learn bookkeeping. She was always proud of her bookkeeping abilities.

The romance between Ivor and Susannah, who became known as Sue, by the English-speaking family; blossomed. She was young and vulnerable and he was ever so dashing and persuasive and thus they were married in Salisbury Cathedral on 28th October 1945. Their first son Hugh was born in March 1946, their second Son Alan was born in May 1949, a daughter Erica was born in October 1953 and the youngest, Tamsin; was born in September 1955.

At some stage in their early marriage, a cruise to Mombasa was taken, evidently for Ivor to share his romantic memories of that lovely town with enviable beaches and the island of Zanzibar nearby. It is an amazing exotic part of the East Coast of Africa. Around that time Susannah who was by then widely accepted to be Sue elected to cut her hair short. Perhaps on account of the heat or an attack of fashion, who knows? Ivor never stopped mourning the loss of that wonderful mane of hair that had so bewitched him.

They acquired a piece of property and built a lovely house on four acres of land. Sue loved gardening and she landscaped the property beautifully. The lovely roomy house and garden were the scene of childhood happiness for the young McCormicks. The large grounds provided many opportunities for imaginative games to be played outdoors. The Holderness family next door were good friends forever and anon. Alan and his friends in the suburb were pranksters causing a fair amount of mayhem. At one time they were apprehended for throwing stones at the neighbours' homes to rattle the roofs. When a window was broken the local policeman arrived to sternly chastise them.

On another occasion, Alan and his friends were playing with matches and succeeded in causing a wildfire in the dry grass on an undeveloped property next door to their house. Later on, where there was a small waterway trickling from a pipe under the road into a ditch dividing their home from the unfortunate piece of land that burned, there was an incident with ducklings. The narrator does not know where the ducklings were originally found, but they were last seen disappearing further and further away from the road and their original home, on the little waterway, as it ran downhill to a large expanse of undeveloped land behind the McCormick property, popularly known as the vlei.

Sue was invited to decorate an office with some potted plants. She was very artistic and her arrangements and fond care of the house plants became the talk of the town. Gradually she was invited to provide more and more green relief in offices and a business called Inscapes was born. Over the years it grew in size and became fairly lucrative. In her spare time, she took up pottery and became very skilled in that activity. Her artistic instincts were increasingly stimulated and she started painting and took art lessons. In later years she started spinning and weaving. Her creative activities were many and varied. She used her hand moulded, glazed and fired pots to display the glossy, green plant foliage, to great advantage in her Inscapes clients' offices.

She became an avid traveller to the East, visiting Vietnam, and Japan and later venturing West to South America, visiting Peru and Lake Titicaca and on most trips, found ways to stop to while away some time, in her favourite artistic haunt in New Mexico; Santa Fé. She had discovered this centre of artistic excellence when for a brief time, her daughter Tamsin was there on assignment. Tamsin later settled on the outskirts of Boulder in Colorado on a mountain pass called Goldhill where she and her husband built an adobe-style house on the side of the mountain looking down on a dense conifer plantation.
At the time they were both serving in Professorial positions at Colorado University as Geologists. Sadly, that house burned down in a forest fire and is no more.

Alan tells the story of a time when Sue had been in Japan, not only studying the language, manners and art but also succeeding in learning to speak, read and write Japanese. From there she posted a large box of her pottery pieces, with available space filled with powdery glazes in plastic bags. At the time Alan was studying in Durban where he met Solveig the narrator. He was in some difficulty collecting the parcel because the customs officers suspected the white powders of being Cocaine. Eventually, he asked the officer to taste the powder which ended the discussion.

Sue also was very interested in various religious beliefs. She dabbled in Eastern theologies and practices in a way that alarmed the family somewhat. She then discovered the Bahai movement which has headquarters on Mount Carmel in Israel. The writer who has other ideas based on Biblical history finds this somewhat curious. Yet Israeli people, having suffered so terribly for their faith have now adopted an open door to all beliefs and since Bahai claims to encompass all faiths there is this massive temple on the crest of Mount Carmel approached by acres of stairs up the hill.

In later years Sue adopted Catholicism and was very close to the "Father" in the local church. She was most undoubtedly completely sincere in all her searching.

Sue genuinely loved growing indoor and hothouse plants. She tended her orchids with love for many years and her garden was magnificent. Her enthusiasm for growing beautiful plants rubbed off on the whole generation and the next. At this point, it is remembered that she was very fond of palm trees. After Ivor passed away, she went to live in England with her daughter Erica, and there she lived to a grand age. For a while, she took in pottery students and also provided greenery at the local library. She also set up a loom in her living room and continued weaving. She eventually passed away quietly in March 2021 shortly after Solveig's sister, Ingrid left this earth on her journey to eternity.

It is terribly sad when an elder passes on and those left behind realise that there remain so many stories left untold. Truly the narrator of this family history wishes there was so much more information stashed away in journals that could be used to fill out the pages of this story as it is being written.

At one time, it is recalled that this indomitable lady, Sue travelled to Peru and journeyed through mountains to Lake Titicaca, met remote Peruvian people and discovered their culture. She came home with photographs of battered and faded old buses, on which she had ascended and descended steep mountain passes made of shockingly rough looking roads. These looked pretty impassable to one who is accustomed to tarmacadam. The bus shared the mountain tracks with all manner of people and animals travelling on foot with mountains of goods on their backs. If only this narrator had taken the time to ask questions and hear the stories that could have been shared.

Therefore; it is one of the writer's quests now in late age, to encourage a rebirth of journaling as a daily habit among all people. Current technology and all the sharing on various applications can never replace the daily handwritten gathering of thoughts, ideas and events of a person's life, that can be enjoyed by the generations that follow after.

Sue was not only an intrepid traveller but as we know, her amazing hands also were never still. Solveig was awed at her first encounter with Sue at the potter's wheel, shaping a vase. She admired the turning table and the strength in the potter's hands as she gently but so firmly pulled the clay up to form the shape. She then pushed her fist into the centre to hollow it out, while firmly curving the bulb of the vase with the other hand. Her coordination was impressive as she was also operating the turning wheel by foot pedal. It was fascinating!

The hands had to be constantly wetted to keep the clay pliable. Then as the bulb took shape, she carefully narrowed her fist, drew it out and started shaping the neck with her fingers, stroking upwards and finally drawing the neck of the vase outwards. The narrator had once worked with clay as an art student and had loved the experience so she begged Sue to teach her. The ever-so-humble lady replied that she was not qualified to teach. This was just a hobby.

Some years later the clay work left the potter's wheel and moved to other methods. She started creating interesting new shapes by rolling the clay into long thin "snakes" and then creating a base according to her chosen shape often rounded, but also softly suggesting the triangular shape, building them into ornamental vessels embellished with leather thongs and other natural decorations such as small clay beads and tablets. For this work, her naturalistic firing and glazing methods developed new textures with a variety of clay polishing and burnishing.

Humbly she submitted one of her creations to an international competition. She was astonished and delighted to discover that she had won a prestigious award and travelled to Europe to receive her prize and the acclaim that went with it. Her works were photographed and published in potters' magazines internationally. Years later the narrator attended a huge exhibition in Cape Town and was tickled to observe the weak imitations of Sue's works that proliferated. There is only ever one original and Sue was the creative who started a craze.

Alongside all of that, she also painted. On a trip to Yosemite, she painted the most beautiful scene of Redwood trees, with the forest floor carpeted by ferns, trapping the sun's rays filtering through the giant trees. The colours were brightly clear and true, and the captured light dazzled! After that, she became involved with the National Art gallery as a patron. Some smaller works of hers were permanent exhibits. Sadly, she became involved with a teacher who ran a gallery of her own and who had a great following of slavish students. As in all periods of art development, there is a "Studio Master" (or Mistress in this case) who runs a school, and whose students are taught techniques via imitation of the master's work. This school resulted in "modern" abstract forms with tinctures, possibly inspired by African earth and bushveld. The narrator is ashamed to confess that she harboured no love of the style, and personally felt that Sue's original work was preferable. Her own lively clear hues, shapes and perspectives; had dwindled under instruction! This is perceived as a travesty of her talent.

As we know, Sue had taken up spinning and weaving which she continued with for many years creating the most beautiful textured and patterned woven works. During the war years, she was always knitting, either socks or warm balaclavas for "the soldiers". Even the narrator managed under instruction to produce an imperfect pair of socks for one of "the soldiers"

It is impossible to do this lovely lady adequate justice. She certainly changed the world around her for the better wherever she was.

## Chapter Twenty-Eight
## Wheels Turn

*"Overall He sees, Over all He writes,*
*are spread the sunbeams of a cheerful Spirit –*
*The light of inexhaustible human love."*

*Longfellow - Hyperion*

Kateryna's family originated in Flekkefjord, Norway. A woman blessed with a copious mane of red-gold hair, she was very beautiful; tall, long-limbed and energetic. Her talents were with words, and she became a journalist.

In Oslo, Leif Hartman-Andressen was born into a family whose father and six uncles owned a fleet of seven tall wooden sailing ships. These were used for whaling, pearling and the occasional transport of passengers to the South Seas. They sailed far and wide to where the whales were found. Some whalers travelling south, would occasionally transport prisoners to Australia where they were expected to open up the country which was rich in minerals.

The same ships partook in pearling on the Northwestern shores of Australia whence they delivered divers in the oyster-rich waters. Already in those days they were seeding the pearls and dropping them into designated oyster beds. They would conclude their journey with whale hunting and the fat collection as well as garnering material for corsetry. Over time, some ship masters preferred to rest in the south seas during the southern winter, by taking shelter in local natural deep-water bays and fjords; of which there were many. Some married local people and evidence of this remains.

The boiling of the blubber harvested from Southern Rights and Humpbacks, over open flames could potentially, and sometimes did result in dangerous fires on board the ship. This horrifying occurrence could result in the loss of lives and even ships. Imagine the sails going up in flames! Even though furled, a hot high flame could ignite the canvas in sea winds.

With the development of iron ore into steel in Pittsburgh, the Americans entered into the whaling industry at a great advantage with their new steel-hulled and rigged sailing ships that were much safer. They were also faster as their steam engines continued to develop, and thus they were not always reliant on wind.

The subsequent generation of whom Leif was a part, were forced by changing times to seek other trades and professions. But in the family home in Oslo, there are paintings of the lovely, tall, wooden sailing ships they were so proud of. Denied his heritage as a ship's Captain, He became indentured to a publishing house where he was learning the trade of a bookbinder.

Kateryna moved to Bergen and found employment at the local daily newspaper office where she wrote and edited copy brought in by the news reporters. Her talent was an ability to capture in words the excitement and emotive value with which to liven up the hard facts of simple daily stories of who did what, where and when. This beautiful positive lady enjoyed the outdoors and walked whenever she had the chance, soaking up the scenery, and observing people and their activities around her. Her senses absorbed information which was stored in crystal bright colour and sound in her retentive mind, re-emerging on the pages of her copy in vivid language. She was a keen observer of human nature and the funny little habits people had. This was reflected in her writing.

Leif was bored. Binding books required focused skills but was repetitive. The excellence of the craft, and skills of the bookbinder, were what increased the value of the book. At that time most books of any value were covered in beautifully cured, soft leather. Titles were engraved in the leather in gilt. The pages of higher priced books had gilt edging. He was a good craftsman. However, the work was dull, and he hungered for more. He too went walking while he was turning over in his mind what he truly wanted to do with the rest of his life.

He was fascinated with words and the images they brought to mind in the reading. He believed that history needed to be recorded and he spent a lot of time reading. He enjoyed sketching in ink, small scenes he observed here and there, as he ambled about drinking in the world around him. We know this because some of his writing was found.

One long summer evening as he walked along the water's edge of Oslo marina, looking at the ships and feeling the pull of distant shores, he hungered for change. On the way home, he picked up a news magazine and there read that the Bergen Weekly News required an assistant typesetter. He thought of this opportunity to add another skill to his repertoire as well as a change of scene. Bergen, on a beautiful fjord, promised a new environment and new people to meet. A whole new life!

Leif responded to the advertisement inviting applications from aspirant typesetters. For good measure, he mentioned how the written word inspired mental images that he was able to sketch in ink. The Editor of the Bergen Weekly was intrigued. Here was a two-in-one offer! The painstaking setting of the type required accuracy and a love of the written word. The type-setter needed to be able to spot small errors in the script and to possess the courage to edit on the spot. The close work with words would inspire possible visual comic imagery to be inserted in the blocks of typing.

Leif presented himself as requested for an interview, and was employed.

However, typesetters work with the presses and not in the office cubicles of reporters and writers. One day it came to pass that Leif was called upon and invited to provide some sketches of a humorous nature for insertion into the columns of a page. The written article had been compiled by Kateryna on the subject of ladies' corsetry. They chatted for a while and her beauty and wit inspired him. Shortly afterwards he presented her with several sketches that were not only discreet but also hilariously entertaining. Delighted laughter resounded in the office. The editor selected a drawing for Leif to engrave in wax, and it appeared in the weekly news. He was finding his feet and learning new skills. His clever sketches became popular and the weekly news regularly included his comic strips giving a send-up of the front-page story to lighten the mood of the growing economic depression.

At Christmas, Leif travelled to Flekkefjord to meet Kateryna's family. The following summer, on a gorgeous June day, they were married at her family home. The groom's family travelled to meet the bride's family and the national costumes of the two regions were worn by all for this lovely festive event.

Leif and Kateryna Hartman-Andressen settled in Bergen, in a small house on a narrow lane up a steep incline. It was a few streets away from the edge of the fjord, yet its position afforded them lovely views across the water to the farms and villages on the opposite slopes. One by one the family grew. For a while, Kateryna was able to continue her work copywriting and editing; and her weekly article which these days also covered a delightful diary of the activities of a young wife and mother, under a pseudonym. However, with the third child, she had to stop working.

For some recent years, the summers had been shorter and the winter cold lasted longer. The perishing cold was not eased during the longer daylight hours of "summer". Snow lay thick on the ground into June and July becoming slush in August leaving the earth cold and water-logged. The usual summer crops although reliant on the long hours of sunshine, struggled because the land was waterlogged, putrid and icy.

All over Northern Europe, this phenomenon was felt. Crops failed and livestock suffered. By late September and October, the heavy winter weather returned. The warm North Sea current was cooler and it affected fisheries. The Scandinavian economies suffered.

Shortly after Mrs Hartman-Andressen birthed her latest child bringing the brood to six, three little daughters and three sons; Leif and Kateryna began to discuss moving south to warmer climes. So many people were moving to the Americas where there were a lot of opportunities. But Leif had heard from the Oslo family that Cape Town on the Southern tip of Africa was a place of opportunity where there was already a growing Norwegian community.

It was a difficult decision to make but it was agreed that Leif would go on ahead, find work and organize a home for them; and when all was in order, he would call for Kateryna and the children. In the interim, she was to move to Oslo and live in the capacious, gracious family home where he had grown up. This she did.

The day Leif sailed, Kateryna and her children waved him au-revoir from the quayside with brave smiles and wet cheeks. Kateryna was holding the youngest, still nursing, in her arms.

Leif sailed ahead and once in Cape Town having survived a fairly hazardous stormy journey, he found the Unitarian church, where Norwegian immigrants met weekly. After that, having established contact, he started a news magazine reporting on events among them and their business exploits, in the close-knit Norwegian community's new world as well as, a sharing of odd news items from

Norway. From Oslo, Kateryna forwarded Norwegian news written with her popular journalistic style. By that time regular mail ships were travelling to the colonies. His descendants have a printed magazine of his that has been lovingly preserved.

Once he had settled in the Cape, he sent for his wife and six children. Courageous and oh-so energetic, Kateryna bundled all their belongings into sea trunks and baskets, and in due time arrived by steamship in Cape Town with her brood. The year was 1892.

Recently a piece of Art Nouveau, an exotic painted plate, that has been in the family for as long as the writer knows; has been identified as being made in Belgium around 1880. Could this have been a wedding gift to young Leif and Kateryna?

Time went by and the children grew, though one little girl sadly did not survive. We have little knowledge of the activities of the boys. There were three of them. One named after his father, Leif, reportedly married and settled in the Eastern Cape, and that marriage produced a famous Tenor, Sidwill Hartman. On arrival in Cape Town, Leif Hartman-Andressen had dropped the "Andressen" from the Hartman name. The other two sons, Paul and Rolf, became political activists. Paul returned to Norway and Rolf remained. The little girl that didn't survive was Helga who passed away due to a childhood fever shortly after arriving in Cape Town. The remaining two sisters, Kristoffa and Solveig married. Both were widowed. Solveig was left childless and did not remarry.

The other, Kristoffa, remarried and the results of the two marriages were a son and two daughters. These then were first-generation South Africans born just before, during and after the first world war. Kristoffa's second husband Paul Hawthorn was a manager for Barclays Bank, and he was sent to open up and manage a branch in Bloemfontein, the City of Roses. The older son John Mitchell had left home and settled in George, a growing young city near the beautiful small harbour town of Knysna, where the wonderful surrounding Yellowwood forests, roamed by elephants, that were so famous, became desiccated.

The two sisters, the younger Brenda and the elder Olga, completed their school years in Bloemfontein. During those years in Bloemfontein Paul Hawthorn was much respected as the Bank Manager which produced in Olga an abiding belief that banking is the best profession to be in. All her children started life working in banking institutions. Paul then retired and he and Kristoffa moved to Seaforth near Simon's Town just about the time the second world war broke out, and later to bought a little house in St James on the coast near Cape Town.

The two beautiful sisters enjoyed the war years spending time on the beach and attending weekly dances at the Navy "Seaman's Club" hall in Simon's Town. Olga often told the tale of the dog called Just Nuisance who would travel with the young people on the trains as the naval officers escorted their dance partners home at the end of the evening. Returning to the naval base the Officers were often the worse for wear and Just Nuisance would nose them awake and herd them off the train on arrival in Simon's Town. Olga developed a fascination for a handsome young German seaman, Helmut; who was sadly rounded up by the British and jailed for the duration of the war on the suspicion of him possibly being a spy.

Some years later, when Olga was working as a proud and exceptionally fast typist, she met and married a typewriter technician named Jack Hayden and went to live with him in Johannesburg; while Brenda married Ivan Robinson in Cape Town. Both sisters gave birth to elder daughters and younger sons. The sisters' younger sons were George Hayden and Stuart Robinson. Olga was widowed and Brenda's marriage sadly ended in divorce. Both of them named their daughters Ingrid, and forever after they were called Big Ingrid and Little Ingrid. Olga's children were older than Brenda's. Interestingly "Little Ingrid" is tall and lean after her father's build and Big Ingrid was slight, taking on Olga's build.

Both sisters remarried. Brenda married Roger Hayden, a Jewish man in Sea Point. There were no children born of that marriage, although Roger had two sons from his first marriage. It is interesting to note that both sisters bore the name Hayden at different times. Olga was newly widowed after Jack suffered a fatal haemorrhage. When handsome Edmund Alexander Jacobs entered her life. She was incredibly relieved to find emotional and practical support for herself and her children. Edmund Alexander was quickly renamed by her as Andre. Some five years later the narrator, named Solveig after her mother's aunt, was born.

We are now looking at the second generation of proudly Norwegian immigrants born in South Africa.

Olga's two older children, Ingrid and George, had a wonderful early life in the small suburb on the outskirts of Johannesburg city, roaming around after school in a safe, carefree environment. About four years after the birth of Solveig the youngest of Olga's children, it was found that her extremely premature birth had resulted in, among some physical issues, one being visual problems and later another being identified as approaching deafness. A prominent eye specialist in Johannesburg, Dr Boshoff referred them to another in Durban, Dr Harry Chait; who was developing what was then groundbreaking eye surgery. So, after a year's preparation, the family moved to Natal. Surgery accomplished and spectacles donned, the process was complete. The children grew, completed schooling and entered a modern-day workforce.

The writer whom you the reader have already met was the youngest and was educated in a series of convent schools at two of which she was a boarder. She developed wanderlust and travelled widely, before settling and marrying in what was then Rhodesia.

Her children Patricia and Sean McCormick, the third generation born in Africa, grew up in what had been Rhodesia and became Zimbabwe. It was a most troubled society but they were fortunate to be well educated and receive tertiary education, providing them with opportunities in the wider world. Patricia seems to have inherited the genetic strain of educators from Caroline and Winifred Cordner. She became a teacher and it has been her life's dedicated work. Sean became a Civil Engineer and travelled to England and Seychelles on contract. While he was Site Engineer on a project in the Seychelles, he met his future wife, Mary Ann Clarke. During his time living on the island, he fell in love with sailing and motorboating. He loved diving and is a keen fisherman. It seems that his love of the sea and boating may be inherited from his Norwegian forebears. His mother always loved sailing, and in her youth, nurtured unfulfilled dreams of sailing around the world.

Now, this is the interesting part; the point of the long build-up to events. Kateryna's great, great-granddaughter Patricia; Solveig's elder child who is a tall young woman, long in the limbs; most intelligent, well educated, and a gifted teacher, is blessed with a copious head of red-gold hair. She is a genetic repetition of Kateryna. She married Lance a man of part Danish descent, thus strengthening the Nordic gene pool. Their children are tall as were their ancestors from Northern Europe.

There came a time when events in Zimbabwe, reached a point that required a difficult choice to be made, to relocate. It is a tough decision to leave your parents and strike out to the furthest reaches to start a new life for the sake of your children's futures. History repeats itself. In every generation there are pioneers.

According to a word Patricia received from God, her husband boarded a flight with a rucksack on his back and boldly flew to New Zealand, announcing on arrival that he intended to immigrate. Impressed with his forthright statement they stamped his passport and told him to go and find work. He did. There have been minor obstacles along the way but on the whole, this young family has made exceptional progress.

After he left, his plucky wife stayed behind and settled all their worldly affairs. She sold everything that was possible to sell and later replace, and several months afterwards, she and her children, with copious amounts of baggage, set off for the new country. It was just as harrowing a journey in modern-day terms, as we imagine the steamship transfer was for her great, great Grandmother Kateryna and her brood. Airport transfers are exhausting with small overexcited children and an overwrought mother. They eventually arrived safely. Her stalwart husband had not wasted any time. In between work shifts, he had found them a home and furnished it however simply, yet with love and attention to the style she enjoys; ready for their arrival.

Left behind in Africa, albeit happily in Cape Town, the young woman's mother realised that the wheel had turned. Kateryna had left the land of fjords in the North Sea of Europe, and come to Africa. Her great, great, granddaughter who just coincidentally is a reasonable lookalike, has left Africa and also travelled a vast distance to the opposite side of the world, to a land in part riddled with fjords and glaciers, having a coastline on the South Island, that closely resembles that of Southern Norway! A move was made from the extreme North in Western Europe to the extreme South, almost touching the dateline between East and West. The narrator was genuinely delighted to comprehend that the Southern part of the Norwegian map resembles the Southern part of South Island, New Zealand, way down in the South Seas.

At the time of writing, they are doing well and enjoying their new land and the outdoor life it offers.

It seems astonishing that one can trace the pioneering habits of families through their generations and family lines, The New Zealanders are a plucky family and impressively active and able. Interestingly, Ivor's great Grandson is determined to be a pilot. Since very early childhood he has been fascinated by everything to do with aircraft and as of October 2022, is currently an Air Cadet in early training.

## Chapter Twenty-Nine
## African Bush

*"Those who walk with feet of air,
Leave no live enduring marks."*

*Longfellow – The wind over the Chimney*

Living in the suburbs and working in the city, Alan yearned for the wild African bush country. In his youth, there had been safari holidays. His years in uniform had been bush experiences. He loved the indigenous trees and wildflowers that conquered the rock-like dry soils, emerging impossibly in parts not at all resembling garden land, triumphantly colouring up the barren land, with delicate petals. The most spectacular of these are the Flame Lilies that appear in several colour varieties, from the palest yellow to red; but the popular one resembles delicate petal flames.

In spring the Msassa forests shoot leaves after the driest of winters, in glorious shades of what might be mistaken for a Northern Hemisphere Autumn. A hillside covered in Msassas might vary from lemon yellows through golden russets and bright oranges into dark plums. The wilderness is always a glorious tapestry of colour and texture in that part of the world between August and November. The trees put on their best shows in anticipation of the hoped-for summer rain. Many an artist has made a living painting these country scenes of Msassa forestation.

In an almost boyish fashion, he loved to explore the land, hoping to spot spoor of wild animals. Walking with his head down and eyes closely scanning the dusty earth, he was always searching for imprints in the dusty soil. This habit had been learned during the war when tracking enemy activity and it was a matter of life and death. Using this skill for tracking wild animals was always of great interest. It takes close attention and focus, to recognise the different prints that various species make and what the time elapse has been since the prints were made. Fresh spoor is sharp and old spoor is soft. This takes keen observation.

A good indication of the presence of a big cat is the recognizable aroma of marked territory. His wife smilingly teased that he could accidentally meet the lion, leopard, buffalo or rhino he hoped to track, face to face and be somewhat surprised. Even though, when on the farm at least, he carried a shotgun in case of need, it always seemed superfluous given the suspicion that he might not see a threat until it was too late. However, she enjoyed learning from him.

Before the purchase of the farm in the far North almost at the Great Rift Valley Escarpment, there were many holidays taken to the Northern reaches of the country, descending into the great African rift valley where the abundant waters of the Zambezi River, guaranteed copious sightings of animals. A wonderful resort called Mana Pools is located below the Kariba Dam. From the earliest days of their marriage, Alan and his family, often accompanied by Ivor, travelled most mid-winters to spend a week or two on the dry river banks where animals flocked to drink.

The camp was not fenced and the ethos which all understood, was that we humans are guests in an animal paradise. This is their home and they were to be accorded absolute respect at all times. All movement was to be calm and quiet and every campsite had a fireplace where glowing embers were encouraged at night to discourage hyenas and other roaming wanderers searching for snacks.

The first of such a safari holiday was taken as a young family unaccompanied by Ivor and occurred after the purchase of a great trailer that could open up on an expanding frame with tented sides. It was Solveig's first ever real "bush experience" and she was very excited about it all. In those days Mana Pools was not as popular as it later became so the little family almost had the camp to themselves. After setting up camp, eating dinner and settling the family to sleep in the tented trailer cum caravan, all was quiet apart from the sounds of hippos on the beach, and distant coughing sounds lions make when on the move.

Solveig was wakened by rattling and clattering sounds just at their camp. Curiosity piqued, she peeped out and saw a most beautiful animal. It resembled a badger. In her ignorance, she thought that since there were badgers in children's storybooks originating from England, that there could not possibly be such a creature down in Africa. Puzzling over this she lay there holding the corner of the tent watching the beautiful animal and trying to figure out what kind it was. It had magnificent thick fur, Shortish Legs and an intelligent face with little rounded ears and a tapered snout. All of these might suggest a small bear. But bears in Africa? Surely not! Also decrying the "bear" suspicion was the magnificent busy tail and the beautiful stripe from nose tip to tail tip, glistening in the moonlight.

Bear or Badger? Neither was possible surely. Said Bear or Badger was most interested in the garbage bin just outside and it also stood on hindlegs to investigate the peering occupant of the trailer-tent caravan. The pretty animal and Solveig were almost face-to-face. She had to find out so she woke the gently snoring husband. Excitedly she told him about the bear (or badger) not wishing to be laughed at for thinking it was a badger. His hoots of laughter woke the children and scared the animal who scuttled a little distance off and turned back to see what was potting.

"Don't you know there are no bears in Africa? That's a honey badger and not to be interfered with, as their teeth are sharp and their jaws are vices!" Didn't she notice the wires securing the rubbish bins? This was because the badgers are scavengers when they are not raiding beehives. "Oh, dear!" Forty years later she still feels the embarrassment of her foolishness.

On that trip, she had two very young children and the youngest was still in napkins and nursing. Alan had a large canvas sheet spread out under the tree in the camp. Thereon the younger child was hoped to contain his crawling activities. Not a chance! He continually had to be lifted so that little paper thorns could be removed from his hands and knees and pretty much everywhere on his tender skin.

At the time of writing, she remembers washing thick cotton napkins in a bucket, and hanging them to dry on a line Alan had rigged up between branches with sunshine breaking through, and the wind assisting the process. In the early mornings after tea and toast, the little family went out game-viewing. It was wonderfully exciting! The animals were plentiful. Gazelles resembling Springbok but of smaller stature, with shorter straight horns, called Impala; were numerous and to be seen grazing calmly, although occasionally they would startle and go bounding away showing the dark tufts at the base of their hind legs.

During July Buffaloes calve, and the herds gather in great numbers on a chosen plain where all the adult males surround the calving females to protect the calves, as they suckle and strengthen. Any predator hoping to seize a calf comes to brutal grief on the horns of the bulls. This great stationary herd observes the humans passing by but intent on protecting their calves, do not break ranks and become a threat to the observers.

The first time this was encountered, Ivor was also there. They paused in the shade of trees and holding the children, quietly watched this amazing spectacle. Ivor went forward and eyed the lead bull letting him know in "wild speak' that he was the head of this little human herd. After watching for a while they moved on. Ivor stayed in a stance of protection for some moments and then quietly joined the family in peaceful retreat. That was a magical experience.

They were fortunate to see this gathering of the buffalo several times though the trips were also occasionally mistimed and the buffaloes were not seen.

Sightings of rhinos were few but there was a watering hole that always attracted hippos in the heat of the day because it was shaded. The glistening water reflecting dappled sunshine and the sparkling spray ejected by the snorting giants was a piece of beauty that is fondly remembered. During the night, hippos gathered on the beach at the edge of the Zambezi and one could hear the peculiar sound of their whizzing tails scattering liquid faeces in fine sprays onto the sand. It was explained to us that their herbivorous diet and copious amounts of water ingested, made faeces fairly liquid, and nature has arranged that this is widely scattered at night into soft dry river sand. Other animals approaching the river to drink in the night and early morning, scuffle the traces, and by sunrise one always finds a clear clean beach. A tiny bit marvellous!

Leopards are nocturnal hunters so it is rare to see one in daylight. They tend to habituate creeks where they can rest unobserved in a shady spot; or on rocky hillsides for the same reason. A dead giveaway is always the presence of a lone, stationary sentinel bushbuck, in an exposed spot nearby. Bush lore is that they have an agreement. Leopards will not hunt bushbuck who in exchange will warn their friends the leopards if there is a possible threat. A regular observer of animal habits will know that where there is a bushbuck there is likely to be a leopard. This does not guarantee a sighting but from time to time one is lucky. It is also known that where there are baboons there are also leopards because leopards hunt baboons by choice.

In a large area inhabited by a variety of wild game, there will be predators. Lions abound, and rivers are full of Crocodiles. Hyenas always arrive where there is a kill as do vultures. Hyenas are known to have the ability to chase lions away from their kills, mid-repast. Cheetahs the fleetest of cats can often be seen being simply still, observing the plains. They can attain fantastic speed on the chase but endurance is poor, so they watch and wait, and choose their opportunities carefully. Yet when they are on the chase, they hardly touch the ground. Wonderful!

Alan and his family often accompanied by grandfather Ivor, and occasionally by Hugh and his wife Liz and family and sisters, Tamsin and Erica visited the game park almost, if not annually, for many years. It became better known and thus more popular. Tourists are not as aware of correct bush manners as "residents" are, and over time the animals became bolder. Hyenas started attacking careless campers and Solveig saw a foreign camper walk right up to an elephant bull with his big fancy camera, planning to "get a close-up shot". She warned him to keep his distance and move slowly and not make a sound. She also warned him that if the elephant charged, he should throw down a hat or a shirt for the animal to vent his anger on. She had read about this.

It happened! The bull elephant took offence, threw up his trunk silently, flapped his ears and stamped his front feet in a warning. She called to the man to walk away calmly and slowly backwards, facing the elephant. But he turned tail and ran, and the elephant charged! That tourist threw his hat down, then his shirt and then his camera, and the elephant trampled all three into the ground. Luckily, he escaped, and no doubt has an exciting bush story to recount.

Elephants delight Solveig. She is fascinated by their vast size and ability to move so silently through the bush. She loves their loping gait on such long legs. Once she had a chance to ride a tame one and was intrigued by their camelid gait. This explains their smooth transition as they move, and she is tickled by their little tails on such vast frames, and their loose skin, creased and crumpled like baggy pyjama trousers.

What we don't notice unless we are up close and personal is that they have very coarse if sparse fur. The hairs are quite long and wiry and each individual hair acts like a cat's whiskers increasing the animal's awareness of its size and position in its immediate surroundings. If not harassed they domesticate and are relatively friendly.

She has learned that they consume four tons of vegetation a day and has been captivated at the sight of them breaking whole tree branches and then folding the lot into mouths with the trunk, and swallowing them without seeming to chew. This is a puzzle. They have these enormous tusks which serve as protection like antelope horns. But she has not seen whether they have molars in their jaws. A quick visit to "uncle Google" has shown that indeed they do have impressive molars hidden in those large fleshy faces.

On one trip a big McCormick family group was all sitting in a semi-circle admiring the river in the moonlight. Ivor had gone to sleep on a camp stretcher under an Acacia tree. They all thought that he was taking a risk but he was calm and confident. However, the years had shown the family that the elephants were very respectful and in the early mornings, it was always evident that they had visited the camp overnight and not disturbed anything or woken anyone. They were quietly chatting in the beauty of the night, when Solveig felt a gentle breeze on the back of her neck. Not thinking of anything else other than a ripple of moving air, she was undisturbed. Until Erica quietly said, "Don't move! You have an elephant investigating your hair". Everyone froze and waited quietly. The great elephant then walked around, passed in front of the assembled family and approached where Ivor was fast asleep.

Alan quietly stood in case it became necessary to do something to extricate "Dad". The elephant reached up to pluck Acacia seeds which had been observed to be their particular elephant delicacy. All waited with bated breath. Then the elephant, whose quest for the delicious seed supper was impeded, reared onto his hind legs and planted his forelegs silently without even causing a rattle in the leaves, against the tree above Dad; forming an elephant arch over the sleeper. Then he noiselessly harvested and ate his fill while the rest of the family watched in awe.

To this day nobody present then knows whether or not Ivor woke and saw the elephant towering over him. Gradually one by one the family wandered off to the shower block or crept into their tents. Alone, Solveig folded and stacked camp chairs and tidied away tea mugs after washing them in a waiting bucket. The elephant had gone. She was not expecting another. She took the corners of the tablecloth and turning around towards the river, shook it to release crumbs. As the cloth flapped, she saw huge white tusks rise up in the moonlight with a startled trunk curling up to the star-spangled heaven.

Her immediate response was to whisper "oh my baby I am so sorry, I didn't mean to frighten you!" The great grey giant turned its head to look at her for a moment and then quietly wandered off. All these years later she relives that moment of wonder and her response to it. And that her calm tone, as if speaking to a child, reassured the majestic beast.

During that trip, Tamsin's curiosity got the better of her. She wanted to know why the elephants literally feast on the Acacia pods. Accordingly, they all started breaking pods open to get a taste. The seeds are delicious but don't tell anyone! They belong to the elephants and the forest.

Animal stories abound in the family as trips to game reserves are a favourite activity.

As with the prolific Impala, the many herds of Zebras are much loved for their unique stripes and upright black and white manes. The stripes on every Zebra are particular to each one, enabling the young to easily identify their mothers in the group. A great lover of horses, Solveig also finds Zebra to be irresistible equines.

On another day Alan and Solveig were canoeing on the river. He had been told that if Hippos appeared, it was advisable to stand up, as his towering height would threaten them and make them move off. It happened. A group of Hippos emerged suddenly in front of the canoe. Alan stood. The canoe rocked dangerously. The hippos sank under the water. A draft of wind tossed his cap into the water and he dropped his packet of cigarettes when reaching to retrieve it. The water current was carrying the cigarettes away which was a major disaster. So, he hopped out of the canoe to go after the cigarettes, leaving a somewhat terrified wife alone in a wildly rocking craft. What about crocodiles?!

By chance, she looked upwards to her right, directly into the collective unblinking feline eyes of a sizeable pride of lions relaxing on the bank just above, calmly watching the antics of the humans in the canoe. The lions must have eaten well recently as they were disinterested and merely spectating. Just as Alan was back in the canoe and trying to quell its violent rocking, while Solveig was pointing out the lions which infuriatingly had slunk off, there was unexpectedly the most beautiful sight of a herd of waterbuck leaping in arcs over the water as they crossed the river. Water sprayed up in showers around them and dazzled with rainbows in the drops. This glorious sight transfixed Solveig. She had recently seen a film documentary of Reindeer in Lapland behaving the same way and had thought it so wonderful. This has remained with her as a preciously special experience. What an incredible chain of spectacular animal sightings that turned out to be!

Another whole book could be written only about Safaris in Rhodesia/Zimbabwe.

There were five-day canoe trips with professional hunter guides and there were white water rafting trips. The five-day canoe trip was something Alan and Solveig badly wanted to do, but there was a minimum number of participants required for the adventure. A group was finally rustled up, consisting of sopranos from the choir. Alan and the two guides were seriously outnumbered. That was a fabulous laughter-filled adventure trip, though we will allow the imagination to dwell on that. The antics of a particularly ribald Australian woman were most entertaining. You the reader, are allowed much speculative license.

Just around that time, Alan took a notion to retire to the country and become a gentleman farmer.

## Chapter Thirty
## War, Rungudzi and Fear

*" At the flaming forge of life Our fortunes must be wrought, ….,
On its sounding anvil shaped, Each burning deed, and thought."*

*Longfellow – the Village Blacksmith*

When Solveig first went to live in Rhodesia by invitation of Alan, she found work with the Public Services Commission and was assigned a post as an Administrative Officer at the Ministry of Local Government and Housing. This was something completely new and different from all her previous banking experience. Every morning a person would dump a few files on her desk. She had no idea what to do with them. But she would read a few of the letters and then compile a reply for the typing department and put the file in her out tray.

Dimly aware that this was providing public service, her conscience "niggled". Such is the boring life of a disinterested public servant. All these years later she has a sudden sympathy for those that are now in a similar position. There appears to be a complete lack of instruction on how to serve the people of a nation.

The country was at war and Alan would be "in the bush" for six weeks on "National Service" and then back to "civil service" for six weeks. As luck would have it, her ministry interacted with his. She felt a certain responsibility, not wanting his fellow workers to think she was letting him down. When she saw him off at the brigade depot, she decided to spend her time alone investigating her role at the office properly. For the next six weeks, she requested twenty files from the registry every Friday and took them home. Nobody questioned this activity. Then starting from the bottom of each, she read through them making notes of the history of each file. What she saw appalled her. The complete disinterest in issues concerning the members of the public requesting service was horrifying.

During the lonely weekends, she examined the requests and complaints; and drafted letters to the incumbents showing interest in their problems, taking care to creatively outline possible solutions for consideration. Every Monday approximately twenty letters were sent through to the typists and then returned to her for signature. This continued until she had been through everything in the departmental registry. Of course, this roused a cyclical procedure, but at least she gained an incremental understanding of the ministerial operation. One particular issue was that of a farmer who was requesting the use of government-owned land adjacent to his farm, by lease, for extra grazing for his beef herd. It was a dry area and his animals needed to roam further in order to obtain adequate nourishment. The replies from various government departments claiming to have rights to that parcel of land simply didn't hold water, and to her, they appeared to be needlessly obstructive.

All mail was addressed to all parties in the discussions. The tone of some of the letters aroused a deep-seated campaigner's heart, that of the girl who went to Israel and lived on the edge while there. She had experienced land reclamation of the desert first-hand and seen the amazing drip irrigation invented there and now used worldwide. What on earth was the problem here in allowing a farmer to use land, that nobody seemed to have a constructive reason to refuse him?

One day, after many months, the embattled farmer called her. Thanked her for her wholesome and continued efforts but admitted defeat. He was packing up and heading for South Africa. It was the beginning of the land use deterioration in Rhodesia, which continued more violently when the country became Zimbabwe!

Time passed. Alan and Solveig married. He was still serving at the time of the birth of their first child. Shortly after the birth he was wounded in action. Two bullets pierced the region of his left shoulder blade and stopped there, fortunately. Doctors removed them and sorted out the burned flesh in the wounds. His arm was in a sling to facilitate undisturbed healing. To make matters worse his mother-in-law, recently divorced was visiting on account of the grandchild, and grousing at length about her aggrieved state. Poor Alan needed regular trips to the hospital for wound dressings. His wife was in a complete state between her mother's demands and the needs of the baby and poor Alan did not get the attention he needed. He felt neglected when he was compelled to drive himself to regular checkups. Only in the writing does it occur to his wife that his father Ivor would have gladly assisted, had he been asked.

His new baby daughter was under the attention of a paediatrician, who had weird ideas, and scared the poor young mother to the extent that now she wishes that she had had the courage to refuse her access to the child. The ultimate horror was inflicting a lumbar puncture on the baby, undoubtedly without the kind gesture of a local anaesthetic, that could numb the insult.

Because the baby was small for dates at birth, the paediatrician prescribed three hourly feeds round the clock. No such thing as demand feeding and allowing the baby to get adequate sleep! She had to produce three winds after every ten-minute suckling session. But the baby never broke any wind! The distraught mother was continuously feeding and encouraging burps, changing nappies and starting again. The poor infant suffered colic and screamed piteously between six and ten every evening for three months while the mother sobbed in sympathy. The whole farce was a nightmare for all concerned. Officially Alan was still in national service, having recently been made a Sergeant. Hardly was he over this hurdle when a Melanoma was identified. It is recalled at this point that in Israel, no man is called into service no matter how dire the situation, during the first year of his marriage!

Alan returned to National Service after dispatching his mother-in-law and when the shoulder wounds were healed. But a doctor in his troop continued to warn him to get the Melanoma attended to. After some time, the "foul spot" was attended to. A large patch of flesh was removed from Alan's chest and the extent of the offending spot was cleared. But there was plastic surgery to close that exposed area. Eventually, it healed and the large scar often raised a question. A sense of humour resulted in the story that the "patch" in front was the point where the two bullets that entered at the back exited. A lot of tender sympathy resulted, and there were secret smiles. Only very recently the narrator was reminded of this forgotten piece of fiction and enjoyed a good chuckle.

Two children were born and nurtured. Solveig became a fortunate home-based mother. Mothering and homemaking made her happy. The war ended and political changes were achieved. Life was good. From time to time, husband and wife shared dreams of farming. However, in each mind, different images were formed.

She envisaged a green valley enclosed by high mountains with a lake or two, a white gabled house, clusters of oak trees, white-painted wood-fenced paddocks for horses and Friesian dairy cattle; with vineyards stretching away in the distance, or at least mixed vegetables, and orchards. This is in keeping with her memories of childhood visits to the Cape.

He was dreaming of great African open spaces, beef cattle and tobacco. Part of this dream was also in the long run to encourage wild game, and have a bit of a game lodge, with rustic chalets for weekend visitors. Somehow these dreams were only dreamed and not communicated to one another in any descriptive sense. They were probably inspired in his part by tales of Chile and Argentina.

She was in Cape Town, with the children visiting her mother, when he called to say he had bought a farm. Lo and behold it turned out to be the very land she had argued over in the Ministry. The owner had left the country as promised, the land had been claimed by the ministry and given to a local man according to the new policy of land resettlement. But the new owner had accumulated debts he could not pay. His venture had failed dismally and he had mentioned to other people in the area that he "wanted out".

It happened that this information reached Alan who agreed to help this man return to a lifestyle he could understand and manage, in exchange for having all his debts settled. The McCormicks were suddenly farmers. When the title deeds were in hand, Solveig recognised the shape from all her Ministry dealings in the area. Attached to the original privately owned farmland, was the portion of state-owned land that the beleaguered "Mr B". had begged to lease, now forming part of the whole property. Three thousand hectares of land that had at one time been used for Virginia Tobacco and Beef production were suddenly Alan's. Her sister Ingrid very humorously made the comment, when she saw the vast wild land: "You have a lot of gardening to do here."

For twelve years he expended everything he had developing the erstwhile wasteland into a beautiful farm. He game-fenced with electric inner wires to hopefully prevent cattle rustling. He built roads and dams, dug boreholes and planted trees. His great pride and joy, was the beautiful village he designed and had built, to provide homes of a relatively unheard-of standard for employees. Other farmers visited, looked and were impressed by his generosity. He bought horses and built stables. His wife and daughter and occasional visiting friends enjoyed long outrides on a collection of pretty thoroughbreds. What luxury! What generosity of spirit!

Alan McCormick's wife and children continued living in Harare at the family home in Greendale. Solveig just could not bear to send her precious little ones to boarding school, having not been a happy boarder herself as a child. Every weekend they travelled to the farm with the vehicle loaded down with groceries and random farming requirements. Sadly, in the interim Solveig had taken over the responsibility of running her mother-in-law's horticultural business, which meant that during the school holidays, she could not be on the farm during the week. This caused a real physical pain in the chest.

Alan's meticulous attention to detail resulted in his tobacco crops being exceptional and attracting top prices. The lifestyles of his farm employees improved and the general mood was of happiness and trust and hope for the future.

Then the narcissistic megalomania of Robert Mugabe turned the country upside down, and suddenly there were hordes of people threatening farmers, and their employees, trying to force them off their land. Alan had gone into opposition politics as an independent candidate for the farming district. Several other farmers decided to join in and support a new opposition party by protest. A meeting was held at the McCormick house in town. The men sat in a circle in the garden sharing their views, their fears and their prospects and in general, whether they were brave enough in the current mood of terror that prevailed. Solveig was there as a hostess, not participating because it was a man's meeting. She served refreshments and silently observed.

Gradually the men came to a unanimous decision that they would resist the current political crisis with everything they could muster, even unto possible death. The silent observer noticed that in the moment the decision was taken, each man's hair greyed before her eyes. Not one of them was above fifty years of age and had not had any grey hair at the beginning of the meeting!

A new constitution had been compiled that on the face of it at first, was a beautiful document. Because of Alan's political aspirations, he brought home a copy for his wife to read. It was a large document and she took her brief very seriously. On page 100, approximately dead centre of the document, she found a clause that enabled Prime Minister Robert Mugabe to unilaterally, with one sweeping stroke of the pen, change anything at all whatever, or however he so wished, at any time, without consulting Parliament.

That small clause completely invalidated the entire constitution. At the time, the document had been put forward for national approval and there was a specified time before a referendum would be held to accept it. It is a known fact that very few people pay attention to this sort of thing and then wonder why they are surprised by further developments in the future.

Solveig morphed into a political activist and threw herself into the project. People had to inform themselves and read it. She collected piles of copies to distribute and begged people to read them closely, in particular concerning the hidden danger on page 100. She went to schools and offices and restaurants handing them out and even boldly walked into a couple of "Shebeens" which were hair-raising. (A "Shebeen" is an unlicensed bar, a place of ill repute, where rather rough people tend to gather). One day, after she accosted a school parent at a bus stop, who identified himself as a "Mugabe man" and parliamentarian, she realised she should tone down her activities. She too was afraid.

Not long after that, Mugabe addressed the nation berating "white farmers" for interfering in politics. He displayed oratory tactics that reminded the viewer of Hitler and Stalin. In that unforgettable diatribe, wearing his narrow Hitler-style moustache, shaking his fist threateningly in the manner of the afore mentioned oppressors, as he expounded; informing the horrified nation, expression glaring with a terrifying threat at the cameras: "I don't care if I have to completely destroy this country and her economy in the process, I will rid Zimbabwe of every single white person." That address to the nation was and remains; an unforgettable experience.

The terror ramped up. Strangely, although his hate was directed at pale-skinned farmers of European descent, the people that took the brunt of it were the African indigenous, the city poor, and the rural people who were hideously tortured and brutalized. Solveig then started collecting statements from people that had been tortured, describing the terrible inhumanities visited on them, which were so gross she cannot describe them here. She would like to, but sensitive natures not accustomed to firsthand horror experiences; should not be exposed to such things. She collected them all and took signed and witnessed copies to embassies begging them to get the news out. When she visited the American embassy and passed through the impressive security procedures, she was allowed to explain her business to a man who identified himself by his first name. He said he was a C.I.A. operative and had an impressive, fat file on his desk. They had been keeping tabs on Alan for years. He took her statement and accepted her pile of signed and witnessed "affidavits" about the tortures. Some embassies were interested and others expressed visible fear and asked her to go away.

The tortures began happening on Rungudzi Estate. Indescribable brutality. One night a loyal farm employee came to the kitchen door shuddering and awash with tears. He had just been forced somehow or other, to stab his brother through the heart. Solveig reached snapping point! If their presence on the land was the reason for this brutality being visited on innocent hardworking people, given that the stated intention was to "get rid of farm owners"; it was time to go. The following morning, she packed up and returned to Harare with the children, never to return to the farm again. Alan remained.

He had worked and invested of himself for twelve years to bring the farm which was his life's dream, to a profitable point. That year he had planted his first ever "cash" crop. He was never able to see it grow to maturity, reaped and sold.

The acts of terror, personal fear, instability in society and general anxiety broke the marriage. Solveig fled to the land of her birth ably assisted by her amazing, generous husband, she set up a new home and began a completely different life in Cape Town.

Their daughter completed Teacher training and went to England to join the man she loved, and ultimately married, and where they lived and worked for ten years. After qualification as a Civil Engineer their son worked first in

Cape Town, then in London and later on a huge project in Seychelles where he met his wife.

Years later, she understood that her husband had lost his wife, his farm, his dreams and his children in one fell swoop. How has this gentle loving person who has never hurt a soul, borne so much loss and suffering; been able to remain the kindly, generous person that he is?

## Chapter Thirty-One
## Canyonlands

*"Whence these legends and traditions,*
*With the odours of the forest,*
*With the dew and damp of meadows,*
*With the curling smoke of wigwams,*
*With the rushing of great rivers,*
*With their frequent repetitions,*
*And their wild reverberations, As of thunder in the mountains?"*

*Longfellow – The Song of Hiawatha*

Canyonlands National Park preserves 337,598 acres of colourful canyons, mesas, buttes, fins, arches, and spires in the heart of Southeast Utah's high desert. Water and gravity have been the prime architects of this land, sculpting layers of rock into the rugged landscape you see today.

Canyonlands Project preserves the natural beauty and human history throughout its four districts, which are divided by the Green and Colorado rivers. While the districts share a primitive desert atmosphere, each retains its unique natural, and geological, characteristics and offers different opportunities for exploration and adventure.

Tamsin McCormick had transferred her activities as a Geologist from Boulder Colorado to Utah. There she became involved in practical teaching of students about the canyons' geological development by taking groups on river rafting tours, mostly on the Green River, where they could all observe and discuss the land formations and rocky deposits.

Together with a local Natural Park Ranger with whom she spent time hiking in the parklands, she became enthused with the idea of also ridding the environment of alien trees that had been planted in ignorance, by well-intentioned people, and which were damaging the local ecology. Her keenly well-trained eye for the wonder of the earth and nature, not only through many years of scientific training, but also as a result of growing up with the McCormick love of wildlife and nature, makes it impossible for her to resist forming a plan to repair the damaged environment. Her passion and amazing intelligence and ability, coupled with her creative talents, are hugely admired, by Solveig. Her observations are always razor-sharp and expressed with a refreshing sense of natural good humour.

In one conversation she shared her opinion that contrary to popular geological thought, she saw herself (at least then) to be in the Creationist Camp and not in the Evolutionary Camp. First prize awarded by her admiring sister-in-law! It is a privilege to be out in nature in her company. Her keen eye identifies details for close observation, such as insects or tiny bits of interesting gravel, that most people don't notice when admiring the grand sweep of the view. She said all those years ago that she believes those canyons to have been formed by about four or five flash floods of great volume and not by millennia of gradual erosion. Applause, please!

On one occasion the two ladies had walked Rungudzi farm and she made the earth come alive as she pointed out land formations and the myriads of different rocky deposits vying for attention everywhere on the ground. The farm is situated on the edge of the Great African Rift Valley. They joked that when the rift finally separates, There would be a beach at the edge of the farm!

The Canyonlands restoration/preservation project she has been involved with, has been focused on removing Tamarind trees. Due to the understanding that these were planted in well-meaning ignorance, which she and her companion in the Park's employ believe are damaging to the environment; the two have agreed to replace them. Over time the removal and gradual replanting of the land, with naturally indigenous to the area, Junipers; has been a long-range project. For years she has been involved with volunteering groups during spring to do this work.

Annually, crowds of young people work with her uprooting Tamarinds and planting Junipers. And her Labrador is there every step of the way encouraging the fun in the sun.

She has also been an assistant guide in the area known as Arches, taking people on hikes, and explaining to them the rock types and how the stunning formations were formed.

How amazing it has been to observe through biographical records and generational activity how this family has made a wide impact on several continents through their love of nature!

The natural theme of the earth's development, vegetation variety, rock formations and animal life has enriched Solveig's experience of life. What a privilege to have encountered the McCormick family and to have become part of it, and have the honour of giving birth to a new generation through marriage to Alan!

After almost a lifetime of admiring each and every member of the family's specific personalities and talents, enjoying their humour and vivid conversational styles, there is an awareness of having been so greatly blessed. It has been wonderful to have a narrow lack of vision and sensitivity, awakened and broadened and developed, by simply having met, and married one member of an exceptional family!

Apart from all the natural and scientific admiration, it is impossible not to share the following little story: Solveig battled a little with post-natal depression after the arrival of her first child. Insecure and anxious, there was a complete unawareness of joyful playfulness, nor imagination about possible stimulation of the baby's senses. Tamsin arrived to meet her niece, bearing the prettiest little crib pillow. Today more than forty years later, the memory of that little embroidered, lace trimmed pillow melts the heart. Even more striking was the cheerful and clever suggestion that the pram sides should be decorated with pretty pictures for the baby to enjoy, instead of simply having to stare at the boring white interior frame, when awake from infant slumber.

Tamsin's capacity to extract the most joy from life is legendary and simply must be recorded. However, she is a private person and was reluctant to be written about for this book. Thus, the record has been circumspect.

# Photo Gallery

Breaking of land on La Elvira, Buenos Aires, Cordner "Estate".

Farmer driving and Percy on horseback watching.

Caroline Eugenie and Edward Ellis Cordner

Sammy Samuels (Right) with Ivor in front and Graham above and behind Ivor (left)

Could this be Andrew Young McCormick?

Winifred Caroline Cordner McCormick

Ivor Ellis Cordner McCormick Left
Graham Austin Cordner McCormick Right - in Dublin

Lieutenant KAR Graham Austin Cordner McCormick

F.O. Ivor Ellis Cordner McCormick

Ivor Ellis Cordner McCormick

and

Susannah Jacoba McCormick

5 44 Salisbury Rhodesia Squadron - Ivor on the right-hand side

Rhodesia Squadron Harvard airborne

Spitfire

## Chapter Thirty-Two

## Peace, Anguish and Joy

*"Full of hope and yet of heartbreak,
Full of all the tender pathos,
of the here and the hereafter."*

*Longfellow - Hiawatha*

As a child I loved stories. At an early age, I was an avid reader and was delighted by the imagery that words evoked. Even today I do not have a television. I prefer to read. What happens in my imagination is more vivid and evocative than anything that can be depicted on screen unless it is a terrible horror story which my sensitive nature avoids by default.

Many years ago, I created a curriculum vitae detailing education, experience, interests, and the hope that when I retired, preferably with a comfortable pension, I could have a little house on the coast, with a garden full of hydrangeas, and be able to spend my time writing and painting.

Working on this book has been a great learning experience. This is a historical biography for which I had only a family tree and a collection of remembered conversations about various members. Of necessity, gaps have been filled by judicious research, remembered conversations and personal creativity. As I am only an ex-in-law, I have tried not to include myself too extensively in the story. But now, this is about the person inside Solveig:

Often while lying in bed on cold winter nights, I hug myself in gratitude while listening to the soporific sounds of rain falling in the dark of the awareness of my soul. Watching droplets sparkling as they are caught in the outdoor electric lights suspended on the roof eaves. I lie staring through the bedroom window as pale clouds scud across the dark weather-clouded sky, underlit by city lights as they shift in the wind. I am consciously aware of the wind soughing through the wet and wind-blown branches, ruffling leaves of many varieties in a garden blessed with many trees. In this kind of winter weather, I thank God for a roof over my head and a comfortable bed. It is good to appreciate one's blessings and be aware of those that are not so fortunate. I feel deep pity for the homeless, huddled under black garbage bags, and/or cardboard boxes, sheltering under bridges and in street doorways.

As I lie waiting for sleep to come, I remember evenings, wandering in the garden and listening to the sounds of the trees. A Bible group exercise that was once given many years ago, suggested walking in the still night-time garden, consciously communing with our Lord God as Adam and Eve had done in the paradise of Eden. The idea was to truly physically discover an experience of the presence of God.

As a person with a hearing disability I have however learned to concentrate on sounds and pitches in my life as a singer, and am intensely aware of natural noises if and when I put my mind to it. On those evenings out "walking with God" my super-aware state astonished me, when I noticed that each tree made its own music in the breeze. Based on the specific shape and texture of branches and leaves, the individual trees all sang their own songs, and I was walking among a choir of nature. This was in the dark when all feathered creatures were snuggled in their nests. The effect was absolutely entrancing and the result was that I repeated my evening garden strolls a good many times after that. Such peace and wonder!

At one time I regularly walked on Table Mountain above Kirstenbosch gardens from where there is access to several contour paths as well as climbing trails. Recovering from illness I was not employed at the time, and the forest and craggy mountain trails held me in thrall. The exercise was therapeutic. I pushed myself more and more physically, in an effort to mend my broken spirit. Nursery Slopes became a favourite and familiar trail. I even once tried the aptly named Skeleton Trail. It was never repeated due to sheer terror experienced during the descent on the swinging chains, which had not really frightened me too badly on the way up.

Constantly challenging myself on these daily mountain walks, I aimed for increasing heights, distances and more difficult paths. It occurred to me to invest in proper boots, which I did. On my first day out in my new boots, I determined to climb the Nursery route to the top and descend via a trail further on, high on the mountain that I had discovered but not explored. It had rained during the night but the morning sun was shining brightly. There was a little mud about and I congratulated myself for having lovely stout boots on my feet. Thus shod, I was undeterred and overconfident as I started up. Streams were gurgling prettily down the ravines, and bright droplets sparkled on forest ferns and trailing vines and other leafy trees. It was a fairy tale of glistening prettiness and I was being silly.

The higher I climbed the slushier it became, and even in my wonderful boots, I was slipping a little. It became more difficult to find firm ground as I walked steeper inclines. Then it occurred to me that perhaps I was taking a grave risk persevering in his way, and should change direction and go down again. I turned to descend and, still happily enjoying the view from where I was, gazing into the valley, which was so pretty in the contrast of dark mud and sparkling foliage with the sunshine lighting up the lower reaches. I was admiring a gurgling rivulet snaking its way down the ravine when I slipped! Well, one foot slipped, while the other was being sucked into slush.

Suddenly I was out of control slithering wildly and grasping at drooping foliage to try and break the fall! To no avail. I could not get a grip on anything. Wet fronds slipped through my fingers or whole plants were uprooted in my grasp. My boot hit an obstacle and over I went, head first into a terrifying tumble, bouncing off rocks and fearing death as I recognised how high I had been, how alone I was; and how badly I could be hurt. Then my knee was caught by a bigger rock and the slithering and bumping stopped.

Pain shot through me and I thought something in the region of that knee could have broken. Carefully, holding onto the "rock of my salvation" I squirmed into a sitting position and started checking myself for injuries. I was only bruised but the knee was very painful. Berating myself for climbing alone so often without ever telling anyone where I was headed, or when I expected to return, it also occurred to me how stupid I was not to even have a phone with me, let alone with a Mountain Rescue phone number saved on it. What a wake-up call!

Carefully I stood. And even more carefully, started to gingerly hobble down. When I gained the contour path, I expected to find it easier, but no. Limping badly it took a couple of hours to complete a distance that should have taken about forty minutes. When I came upon a bench I sat to rest. That's when I noticed that during the fall my mother's gold locket bracelet had been torn off my wrist. It was so dear to me. Losing it was painful; a shaft through the heart.

It was ten years since her death and in that time, the sheer shock had prevented the shedding of any tears. I had been locked in a terrible dull numbness. This precious memorial of her was irretrievably lost, just as she was. The numbness shattered and sensitivity returned! It had to happen.

The screams tore through me, a rising crescendo of pain howling through a trained singer's throat and the pent-up rage escaped me, fueling the yelling until I fainted again. We'd had a head-on collision with a berserk eight-ton lorry, that should not even have been on that road let alone heading straight for me, weaving around on the wrong side of the road, completely out of control. In heavy traffic, there was no escape. There was glass and blood everywhere. Pain consumed me.

My marriage was failing, I had completely failed as a human being, and my efforts to succour my elderly parents had resulted in this huge massacre. Failed over and over again! All my best efforts had come to this disaster. It was too much to bear! Slipping in and out of consciousness I became aware of mechanical noise and rescuers strapping me onto a stretcher and then the stretcher being lifted. In my confused state, I dreamed that I had fallen from some great mountain, like the Eiger North Face, and was being airlifted out by helicopter. But in reality, it was the "jaws of life" unfolding the car wreckage off me, and paramedics extricating me. Where were my children? Where were my parents?

Surfing in and out of consciousness I became aware of my clothes being cut off me. My new jeans!! Oh no! Thank heavens my underwear is respectable. Oh, dear! There goes my brand-new bra. I was covered by a blanket or something. People were murmuring around me. Someone said: "Do you think she is blind?" Since I couldn't see anything, I supposed I was.

Then someone said: "Do you think she might be paralysed?" Holy moly! In the books, the patient in this situation moves a foot to find out. I tried to wiggle my toes but nobody seemed to notice.

I heard my husband's voice say: "I want the best plastic surgeon to attend to her face". I wondered: "why? What do you care?" (At that time for many reasons imagined or otherwise, I was convinced that I was no longer loved.)

More of nothing. Then I was being hefted around on a metal slab presumably for an X-ray but the pain in my arm was beyond belief and I screamed. Someone said: "give her another shot for pain." I couldn't see, but clearly, I could hear.

I woke in a ward. The parish priest and my husband were there. I opened my eyes and saw them both. From the way Tim Neil sat down next to me, I knew he had bad news. He said he had come to pray with me. My question was: "My parents didn't make it?" He said "Well, the doctors have said you are not strong enough to cope with the shock, but since you already know instinctively; no, they did not make it; and I am so sorry. Let's pray."

After he left, A man with massive bolt cutters came to cut my lovely rings off my wedding finger. I tried to resist but apparently, it was necessary because of the extreme swelling. I was afraid I might lose a finger or two in the process. I might have fainted again because that is all I remember.

Sometime later, I was moved by ambulance to another hospital where the surgeon had managed to book a theatre. My left arm had been smashed and needed pinning and plating. Then I was wheeled into the theatre. Mozart was blaring from a music centre and the medics were dancing. I was amazed! They told me they always had music when operating and they were dancing for joy because God had allowed them to help Him in the hallowed work of repairing broken bodies. He put my shattered arm back together. This amazing Orthopaedic Surgeon needs to go down in history, for the wonderful talent and devotion he displayed in his work. He is Dr Bowers and as far as I know, he still operates in Zimbabwe. Finally, when the effects of severe concussion allowed, a double funeral was held.

The church was filled with flowers as well as a surprising number of mourners. I was wheeled in and parked at the back, still attached to a drip containing a cocktail of pain and antibiotic medicine. I remember a particularly sensitive soul asking me how it felt to have killed my parents!

For some light relief, I return to nature for its soothing effects. The accident happened in my old life. Now I live in Cape Town having fled the horrors of Zimbabwean politics and terrorism. This wonderful space of my new life teems with beauty. My stated delight in walking mountain trails, In forests and along the sea, remains. Sensory delight can hold me endlessly at a promenade barrier as I inhale sea scents and gaze at sparkling light rippling on the water. I peer downwards enthralled by the swirling sea foam frothing in bridal lace constantly forming and reforming. The sea birds swooping and calling and strutting on rocks are a delight. I often visit various beaches simply to gaze at the constantly moving water, changing colour as the sun moves across the sky. I am reminded that the sea is like music, its hidden beats living like a human heart and never stopping during the course of life's performance.

Shortly after the mountain fall, a final accumulation of grief and loss of so many things held dear, family members and a way of life, the terror of the farm invasions, and horrible politics during which I was a bold activist, resulted in a series of emotional breakdowns. In therapy, it was art and story writing that helped me the most. The ultimate blessing of three weeks of daily grief counselling sessions finally released a steady flow of painless tears, coursing unchecked down my face, without any sense of shame and failure. Deep respect, for the husband I ran from, was restored. I began to understand my twisted perceptions and how they had enclosed my heart in a block of ice for so long. It has taken twenty-two years of personal examination to understand how it feels to be a man. How it is to be a soldier, still serving in a war-torn country when he has to take upon himself the responsibility of a wife and a family. What it is to saddle oneself with that responsibility, when there is a possibility at any time, that your life could end in battle contact!

He took huge business risks with courage that I have only now recognised. He started his own Quantity Surveying Practice and then later partnered with an associate to develop a valuable business park.

I have considered how a man might feel when his new wife has no concept of her husband's experience and therefore retreats from him in fearful misunderstanding, feeling rejected and in turn rejecting. And in hindsight, I have recognised the amazing generosity of spirit and self-control with which he handled his situation. I see how senselessly cruel I was without realization of it. In my heart, I believed the whispers from other wives in the district of infidelity, which I now suspect, may have simply been jealous, spiteful fabrications, but, at the time, they pierced me to the heart. A lifetime of misunderstandings build one on top of the other. Plunging into selfish desperation and depression, I was lost.

And he remained ever a gentleman, kind and generous, though on occasion he pleaded for understanding. The pleas fell on a hardened selfish heart. His response was to provide me with a home in Cape Town and release me. I packed up and left. He insisted on escorting me to the border. Whereas in previous journeys I had travelled the first leg to the border between Zimbabwe and Botswana, en route Cape Town between midnight and dawn, on this trip, he insisted we travel in daylight. We left later than I wanted to. He had a plan. As the sun set, he overtook me and flagged me down. "Follow me from here". What else could I do? We arrived by a winding dirt road at the entrance to a quaint bush hospitality spot. There was a magnificent candle-lit dinner served in a private dining room. Champagne flowed and the meal was top class though I do not remember what we ate. Probably, Filet Mignon.

Then we were led to the most romantically furnished bridal suite. I was confused and appalled. Here I was leaving a man whom I thought did not love me, yet he had out of the blue, demonstrated a romantic nature I never suspected existed. In the process of walking away from a marriage I thought had ended, I recoiled from this expression of romance, such that I had never experienced before. Oh, what a metaphorical slap in the face I delivered!

The following morning, we continued on to the border. I drove through the gate and it was closed between us. We stood on either side of the fence looking at each other and bid our farewells. My heart felt like it was torn out of my chest but I grimly continued on the journey.

It was a nightmarish drive. The border experience was hideous. The heat was interminable. Not far into South Africa, I had a wheel blowout. Two police officers lazing in the shade of a fly-over bridge, watched as I unhitched the trailer, unpacked the storage compartment of the car to reach tools, and then tried and failed to operate the jack. This was in the midday heat and amid certain anxieties relating to the activity of the day, I was panicking just a little. Then a car loaded with a large, lovely Indian family stopped; and the driver came to help me. My gratitude could not be quantified. The journey wore on. I joined five-lane traffic on Johannesburg's ring road in late afternoon rush hour traffic. Accustomed to the easily manageable traffic of a relatively small town, it was simply terrifying. But I have lived to tell the tale.

Missing the turn-off to where I had planned to search for overnight accommodation I continued grimly in the dark and pelting rain with a continuous stream of approaching heavy transports, blaring lights in my eyes. Eventually, at around midnight, I spotted a twenty-four-hour service station boasting a superette. I staggered in, and seeing that unbelievably there were customers there, I yelled loudly: "Does anybody know where I can sleep? I have been driving from Zimbabwe." There was a shocked silence as time seemed to stand still.

A kindly gentleman came to my assistance. He knew a farmer who took in overnight guests. "Follow me!" he said, after making a call. What kindness! In the morning my rescuers refused payment and wished me well as I continued. In my home hangs my painting of their house, made in fond memory of their kindness.

## Chapter Thirty-Three
## Gratitude

*"Something within her said,*
*"At length thy troubles are ended."*

*Longfellow - Evangelina*

Time is a succession of days, nights, weeks, months and years filled with events. We meet people and have conversations. A person will say something that sparks a memory and stories are exchanged. Over time people who regularly converse learn a lot about one another and in the course of sharing philosophical opinions teach one another about relationships and life in general. Constant exchange of ideas over time is a learning process. Life is not stagnant. We grow daily in our awareness of the world around us and the relationships people develop with one another.

Through regular thoughtful ruminations, I have grown in understanding of the horrors my dear husband has experienced. My respect for him has increased in manifold leaps and bounds. I acknowledge how carelessly I treated him, and how my leaving the way I did was only one part of the shocking losses he experienced in a very short space of time. He lost his farm. His wife fled and both children left the country in natural pursuit of their futures. How did he survive this amongst the beatings and incarceration at the hands of the ruling party bullies?

I never truly understood the courage that it takes a man or woman to be an entrepreneur, to create a business operation and trust that with hard work it will succeed. The perseverance when there seems no hope of success in sight, the belief in a good reward for efforts. Alan not only started a private practice Quantity Surveying, and found a creative way to pay off the house in record time, but he also designed and built an office block that at the time was the largest in terms of the accommodation offered, in town. That speaks of courage and far-sightedness. And then he bought a farm that had reverted to virgin bush and started that from scratch too.

In part, the writing of this book is an act of penance. Writing is cathartic. Psychiatrists have nothing on this pursuit. It dawned on me one day, that my Medical Aid was more or less being swindled by certain medical professionals who purported to be fixing up my mental instability. Nonsense!

What I needed was a spiritual revelation. One evening I had sunk into one of my "dark pits of self-pity". Strange as this may seem to the uninitiated Christian, I was slumped on my couch musing on the "mess of my life and its hopelessness" and thinking that the easy way out was death. I was thinking I had had enough of life and started planning how to end it all. (This has over time, occurred often.) BUT!!! On that night, a still small voice spoke audibly in the dark and the message that came to me was "You are enough!" I knew it was the voice of God without a doubt.

"What? What does that mean?" Then I remembered having purchased and read a book written by Rick Warren. At the time it was all the talk. It is called: "A Purpose Driven Life". Sitting in the darkened room I pondered on whether I still had it somewhere. I stood up and turned towards the nearest bookshelf. I kid you not! One book had fallen out onto the floor of its own volition. It was Rick Warren's book. Is your hair standing up yet? I picked it up and switching on the lights opened it with a view to reading it. It is a forty-day Bible study of great power explaining the meaning of the Christian walk.

I have always believed myself to be a Christian. Attending church regularly for most of my life I also immersed myself in choir singing which apart from the joy of the music, also strengthens your awareness of Biblical text through the wonderful Wesley hymnals and plainchant Psalms. Yet by the time I had completed the Rick Warren study, I was changed. Having for certain reasons not been attending church for a time, I resolved to resume the practice and in short, also experienced Baptism by full immersion.

That was about four years ago. Regular Bible study and daily devotions, not to mention personal preparation for the sought-after experience of Baptism, brought me from prayer to confession and contrition. The perception of my wickedness on the path to redemption somehow opened my eyes to the fact that my poor maligned husband is a very reluctant hero in the true sense of the word. He never seeks thanks or recognition. He does what he does because it is the right thing to do. This man has no ego. He has diligently supported me ever since the divorce, far more generously than the master of the court instructed. My gratitude is without bounds. I could not have gotten this far without his help.

In the course of my daily prayers, I pleaded with God to bring happiness and fulfilment into his life. I prayed for repaired relationships and mutual respect not only between us but between him and his current family members. When you are using the Lord's Prayer thoughtfully and regularly, an understanding grows of the need for forgiveness before being forgiven is possible. When one is struggling with a bitter heart and therefore the matter of forgiveness, the way to overcome the problem is to simply beam thoughts of love towards the object of the exercise.

The miracle has happened. We have been talking. Recently we have been speaking regularly to one another, sharing daily practical affairs. Wonders never cease! Joy is a simple word but when it enters your life you radiate a glow that others comment on. My life which was a rollercoaster of depression is now a joyful experience. I don't need psychiatric drugs and therapy. All I needed was a God-given husband and a personal forgiveness experience.

Recently the McCormicks gathered together in Kenton-on-Sea in the Eastern Cape. Alan's brother Hugh organized and hosted it in his inimitable style. We all caught up on each other's lives. Thank you, to Hugh, Elizabeth, Darryn, Kim and Ryan and Alan and Erica and Keith, Tamsin, Sean and Mary Anne and all the grandchildren; for the wonderful interlude and chatty sessions around delicious meals.

The repairing of family bonds has meant all the world to me. Some of you have not been featured in this book simply because it started with Ivor's diaries and developed from there into a tale of ancestry, based on fractions of stories I had heard over the years. Graham Andrews, a cousin I only met once so long ago that I could not even remember having done so, has patiently supplied me with photographs, information and family trees which have resulted in this book. When I lost my way and confusion reigned supreme, he patiently helped me to correct. Thank you all for accepting me into your number.

## Author Biography

Solveig McCormick née Jacobs was born in Johannesburg, South Africa, in 1955. The family moved to Durban and settled in a small seaside village known as Umhlanga Rocks.

She was schooled in a series of Dominican Convents as her parents moved around as a result of her father's employment contracts. She has a brother George Hayden and a sister Ingrid née Hayden – Lock – Gunther, now deceased.

Solveig was married to Alan McCormick in Rhodesia (now Zimbabwe) after spending some years in Israel and travelling extensively in Europe. They have two children, Sean and Patricia, both married, and four grandchildren.

She currently resides in Cape Town close to the mountain, surrounded by beautiful trees, where many varieties of birds, flit around joyfully, feeding and nesting. She enjoys gardening and her small balcony is filled with a variety of beloved plants.

www.ingramcontent.com/pod-product-compliance
Lightning Source LLC
Chambersburg PA
CBHW020923090426
42736CB00010B/1009